Hank the Tank
Activity Book

Carolee Dean, MS, CCC-SLP, CALT

based on

Hank the Tank: Animal in the Spotlight

by Carolee Dean

A HOT ROD Decodable Book

Level 2

Digraphs, Trigraphs, Combinations, n(g)k, & Closed
(Short) Vowels

Find the Scope & Sequence for the Series at

www.wordtravelpress.com

Word Travel Press LLC - Littleton, CO

HOT ROD – **H**igher **O**rder **T**hinking
through the **R**eading **of D**ecodables

WORD TRAVEL PRESS

prepare for a reading journey

Copyright © 2023 by Word Travel Press LLC

Littleton, Colorado

ISBN: 979-8-9874895-4-3 (paperback)

Library of Congress Control Number: 2023911730

For information, questions, or additional permissions, address Word Travel Press at info@wordtravelpress.com.

If you would like to share this resource with friends or colleagues, please ask them to visit www.wordtravelpress.com.

Book Cover Design for *Hank the Tank: Animal in the Spotlight* by 100 Covers

Graphics have been purchased and/or authorized for use in this product. You may not resell or share without the permission of the graphic artist:

https://Thenounproject.com

https://pixabay.com

https://www.canva.com/

A Perfect Blend by Amanda Newsome

Contents

Contents

Contents

About the Author

Direct questions or comments to:
info@wordtravelpress.com

Carolee Dean, MS, CCC-SLP, CALT is a speech-language pathologist and certified academic language therapist specializing in the treatment of dyslexia and other language-based learning challenges. She is also a children's author of award-winning young adult titles with commercial publishers: *Comfort* (Houghton Mifflin), *Take Me There* (Simon Pulse: A Division and Simon and Schuster), a YALSA Quick Pick for Reluctant Readers, and *Forget Me Not* (Simon Pulse), a novel in verse. She is the author of the educational resource - *Story Frames for Teaching Literacy: Enhancing Student Learning Through the Power of Storytelling* (Paul H. Brookes Publishing Co.).

Dean has combined her love of children's literature and her passion for helping struggling readers to create the HOT ROD Series – **H**igher **O**rder **T**hinking through the **R**eading **o**f **D**ecodables. The purpose of the series is to provide older struggling readers with meaningful text that connects to the curriculum. Because of her background in language development and speech-language pathology, each book is accompanied by activities to foster growth in all the components of reading as well as language development and articulation. For additional resources see the information on the next page.

HOT ROD - Higher Order Thinking through the Reading Of Decodables

Additional Resources

The illustrated chapter book, *Hank the Tank: Animal in the Spotlight*, may be found at https://www.amazon.com/ in hardcover, paperback, or e-book formats. Hardcover and paperback versions may also be ordered from Barnes & Noble or your favorite local bookstore. Watch the website at https://wordtravelpress.com/ for book news and information about the Audible version coming soon. Sign up for the newsletter. You will need the chapter book for most of the activities in the *Hank the Tank Activity Book.*

The engaging black-and-white illustrations provide students with the experience of reading a real book. It may be sent home for fluency practice. Students may enjoy owning their own copy to read again and again. If sending the book home, be sure to include a copy of the page that explains the Pair and Share Reading Strategy.

Boom Cards The target word flash cards included in this packet are available at no cost in an online format at Boom Learning where you may set up a free account. Some of the other games have been turned into Boom Cards that may be played online. Some are free and some are available for a small additional fee. Go to https://wow.boomlearning.com and explore **Store>Word Travel Press.**

Story Frames for Teaching Literacy is available through Brookes Publishing or Amazon. It explores text structure in depth and comes with over 35 adaptable lesson plans and downloadable activities.

DOWNLOADABLE PDFs & Games

The activity pages in this book may be printed for student use. Do not distribute these pages at large. Purchase of this book also includes access to the Activity Pages PDF Download. The Purchaser's Code for the download is intended for purchasers of this activity book and is found in the **Downloads & Online Resources** section near the end.

Find additional books and resources as well as the scope and sequence for the HOT ROD series on the website at www.wordtravelpress.com. Go to the CONTACT page and scroll to the bottom page to sign up for the monthly newsletter to keep up with book news, articles, and free activities.

Decodable Chapter Book

Plot Analysis

Digital Boom Cards

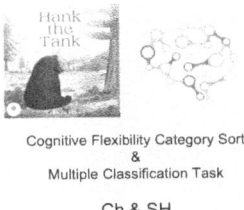

Cognitive Flexibility Category Sort
&
Multiple Classification Task

Ch & SH
Foods & Actions

Target Users

The chapter book, *Hank the Tank: Animal in the Spotlight* aligns with Level 2 of the HOT ROD Series- Higher Order Thinking through the Reading of Decodables. It was written for older students and even adults (grades 4 and up) who still need work on decoding words that contain digraphs, trigraphs, and combinations. The extensive background information included in the book makes it appropriate for use with general education students as well.

This Activity Book includes flash cards for word work along with numerous activities that focus on the Components of Reading (COR) that support reading comprehension and writing. Go to www.wordtravelpress.com to find the Scope and Sequence of the series.

Students with a sixth-grade reading level or higher may read the entire chapter book independently including the Background Information section. Younger students and struggling readers may listen to the text read aloud and read the story poem themselves with support. Find out how to support each reading level on the pages for Reading Levels and Supports. Accommodations are provided for grades 2 and up.

Books from the HOT ROD Series can be used to supplement any reading program but were specifically designed to support Orton-Gillingham based instruction. Level 2 may contain more elements than are traditionally taught to beginning readers. That is because these stories and poems were designed as a review and consolidation of concepts. They are also intended for older readers who often have a higher sight word vocabulary than younger readers as well as more exposure to suffixes and prefixes. The story may be used at any point after all closed (short) syllable sounds from Level 1 and digraphs, trigraphs, combinations from Level 2 have been introduced. It is intended to reinforce those concepts.

Pair and Share Reading

Pair and Share Reading is a strategy incorporated in the HOT ROD series that *pairs* developing readers with proficient readers (educators, parents, peers) who *share* the literacy experience by reading the more challenging segments of a text aloud while the developing reader reads the portions that are targeted for their decoding level. The text for *Hank the Tank* may also be "paired" with the audio recording of the book when that becomes available. Watch the website for details.

The reading partner may be a reading interventionist, speech-language pathologist, or other educator working 1:1 or in a small group with students. In the classroom, teachers can more strategically assign portions of books to be read aloud by students at very different reading levels. They may also pair struggling readers with more advanced ones to work together as reading partners.

The stories from the HOT ROD series are perfect for parents who want to support the reading instruction happening at school or other settings. The books can be sent home for additional reading practice or parents may incorporate them on their own in consultation with a teacher, therapist, or reading tutor.

Finally, homeschoolers may use books from the series along with the Pair and Share strategy to provide reading fluency practice and to introduce their children to content at or beyond their current reading level. In fact, exposure to rich content is at the heart of the strategy. The activities may be used to work on a variety of skills across age and ability levels.

For information about the Scope and Sequence of the HOT ROD series and to find additional titles, go to https://wordtravelpress.com/.

How to Use This Resource

Scope and Sequence - Look at the scope and sequence to make sure the story aligns with the student's current decoding level. If not, words that contain unfamiliar patterns should be pre-taught as learned words.

Practice Reading Target Words – Patterns targeted for Level 2 are digraphs, trigraphs, and combinations (**ck, ng, sh, th, ch, tch, qu, wh,** and single consonant **n(g)k**). If students need additional practice with closed (short) vowels or consonant blends, see the books from Level 1. Practice the Target Word Lists in this resource to make sure the student is accurate 90% of the time before they read the story poem. If needed, students may practice the Words-In-Sentences in the Dictation activity prior to reading the story.

Learned Words - Learned words must be taught prior to reading either because they contain an irregular pattern or because they include a pattern that has not yet been taught. If the student is not familiar with these words, practice them using the Copy & Memorize strategy described later in this resource.

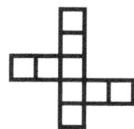

Pre-teach Vocabulary – Introduce the vocabulary terms from the story before reading. Do the same for the vocabulary terms that go with the Background Information section.

Access Prior Knowledge – Before reading the story, share prior knowledge about bears through a class discussion. Have students discuss their preconceived ideas and beliefs about bears that break into houses. Make a list as a class. Prepare them for the fact that some of their ideas may prove to be true and some may not.

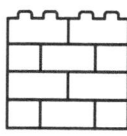

Work on Component Skills – Students often struggle with reading because of weakness in underlying skills other than or in addition to decoding. This resource is filled with supplementary materials to work on phonological awareness, morphology, vocabulary, cognitive flexibility, sentence structure, written language, and more. Pick and choose the activities that best support your students' current needs. See pages 14-15 for a description of each of the 11 categories and 50+ activities addressed in the Activity Book.

Data Collection – See specific directions for calculating fluency. For activity pages, simply divide the number of correct responses by the total number of possible responses for a % correct. Boom Cards may also be used for data collection.

Collaboration – Classroom teachers, reading interventionists, and speech-language pathologists may easily collaborate to explore different activities based on the same content. Each professional may use the activities that support their goals and objectives for a particular student or classroom.

Reading Levels & Supports by Grade Level

Grades 6+ - Students and adults with a reading level of 6.4 or higher should be able to read the entire book independently. Encourage them to study the key terms first. The information can then be used to work on written responses and higher-order thinking activities. Prior to reading, make students a copy of the PAGES Strategy and instruct them on its use.

Grades 5- Students at a fifth-grade reading level may read the entire book with instructional support after vocabulary terms are formally introduced. They may need help parsing longer sentences. Question them often and have conversations to check for understanding. Walk them through the use of the PAGES strategy and provide opportunities for practice.

Grade 4- Students with fourth-grade reading skills should start with a discussion of the vocabulary terms. They may read the decodable story independently but should listen to the Introduction and Background Information read aloud unless they are reading above grade level. Focus on using these elements of the PAGES Strategy: Pause and Picture, Ask, Go Back. Incorporate other elements as students are ready.

Grades 2 & 3 - Students with skills at grade levels 2-3 may practice reading the Target Words and Learned Words aloud. If accuracy is above 90%, they may read the decodable story with support after listening to the Introduction. If accuracy is below 90%, they should continue practicing the target words and the sentences in the Dictation section until they can read them with ease, or they should listen to the story being read aloud. Read the Background Information to them as time permits. Introduce the concepts of visualizing and self-questioning from the PAGES strategy.

Level 2 Decoding (Use with any grade)

Regardless of age or grade level, students working at decoding Level 2 of the HOT ROD Scope and Sequence (found at https://wordtravelpress.com) or a similar program should follow the steps below:

1. Practice reading the Target Words and Learned Words to 90% accuracy or higher.

2. Listen to an explanation of the Key Terms.

3. Listen to the Introduction read aloud. For greater independence, students may

   listen to an audio recording of the book if available.

4. The student reads the Decodable Story out loud to a reading partner.

5. The student listens to the Background Information read aloud using the PAGES Strategy.

6. Discuss the HOT TOPIC questions.

Copy and Memorize Strategy

Decodable books and stories use words based on syllable patterns that the student has been strategically taught, but they typically also contain some phonetically irregular words that cannot be decoded. These words only make up about 5-10% of the English language, but they occur frequently in books and in spoken language. Their use should be limited ideally to 5% of a text or less in decodable books. We call these words **Learned Words**, though other programs may use different terminology. They need to be pretaught before reading a decodable book using the steps below. In addition, if a text contains words that are regular but based on patterns that have not yet been introduced, they should be taught as learned words for the text to be considered decodable.

Say – Say the word out loud and have the student repeat it.

Copy – Have students copy the word from a model, naming each letter as they write it. End with saying the whole word out loud again. Start with near-point copying with the word next to where the student is writing. Evolve to far-point copying with the word on a whiteboard five or more feet away. They may also start with tracing the word that someone else has written and then make a copy next to it.

Check – Instruct the student to check to make sure they have copied the word correctly. If not, repeat steps one and two.

Study – Look at the parts of the word and determine what sounds are spelled in an unexpected way.

Copy – Copy the word again. Start with saying the word out loud. Copy it naming each letter. Say the word again after it has been written.

Memorize – Cover the word and write it from memory. Tell students to name each letter as they write it and end by saying the whole word out loud again.

Check – Uncover the word and check for accuracy. If needed, repeat the steps.

Fluency and Accuracy

Repeated Readings – Reading a text multiple times has been shown to increase fluency and accuracy. Many of the stories in the HOT ROD Series incorporate poetry which naturally lends itself to repeated readings. In addition, because the stories include engaging and high-quality content, students are excited to circle back to the stories as their decoding skills improve when they can read the entire selection independently. The Scavenger Hunt Activities were designed to promote rereading as students search the text for clues to solve a word puzzle.

Reading Fluency and Miscues - While the student reads aloud from the chapter book, tally errors. This may be done on a piece of paper by creating hash marks. Each page has a word count in greyscale at the bottom. If you want more detailed information about what types of errors students are making, errors may be coded as follows: SC= self-corrections, I = insertions, R = repetitions, O = omissions, S = substitutions, and D = delays of more than 2 seconds.

Calculate Accuracy –
Total Words Per Page – Errors = Total Correct.
Total Correct ÷ Total Words Per Page   = % Correct

Prosody – To work on prosody (patterns of stressed and unstressed syllables) see the activity called *Feel the Beat*.

Components of Reading Overview

Note: The HOT Topics page at the end of this Activity Book explains how the activities listed below fit into the 24 categories of Bloom's Revised Taxonomy. The icons to the left are found on the activity pages that support that skill.

Decoding & Articulation Practice and Pre-reading:

Target Words – Read each column of words as a preview before reading the story. Tally errors and calculate a baseline based on the number of words in each column. Retest after reading the story and completing the activities of your choice. Sentences are available for additional practice for one syllable target words on the Boom Cards and in this book.

Learned Words – Practice the Copy & Memorize Strategy.

Phonological Awareness:

Say It Again, Sam - Students work on deletion by repeating words and leaving out sounds or syllables.

Sound Tracks- Students change one sound at a time to create new words

Feel the Beat – Underline stressed words in the poem and practice reading with prosody and stress.

Rhyme Time #1 – Circle rhymes, underline alliterations, and write a sentence containing an alliteration.

Rhyme Time #2 (Part One)– Come up with words to complete a poem following a pattern of stressed and unstressed syllables.

Rhyme Time #2 (Part Two) – Create lines of an original poem.

Cognitive Flexibility:

Category Sort & Multiple Classification Task – Sort words by phonological features (SH & CH). Sort the same list according to semantic features (Foods & Actions). Then use a four-square grid to sort all 4 categories simultaneously. This is a FREE Boom Card Activity.

Morphology:

Morpho Mania – Suffix **ING**, Prefix **RE**, Root **TRACT**. Study the words. Then play a matching game. Explore how sometimes words with ING are verbs and sometimes they act like adjectives.

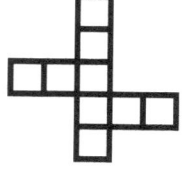

Vocabulary:

15 different activities explore words before, during, and after reading. Students learn strategies for using **Context Clues** to understand word meanings. They create **Vocabulary Foldables** for target words and use them to play **Matching Games**. They learn **Idioms** and **Multiple Meanings**. During **Scavenger Hunts** they reread to find words.

Written Language Overview

Sentence Awareness and Sentence Construction:

Sentence Mania - Explore helping verbs and learn how verbs can be used as adjectives.

#1 Sentence Combining - Combine short sentences into longer ones using the coordinating conjunctions provided.

#2 Who is Doing What? – Answer questions to build sentences.

#3 Identifying Complete Sentences – Judge if sentences are complete or incomplete. Decide which part is missing. Write a complete sentence.

Plot Structure, Story Retells, & Summaries:

Story Frames – Students complete a storyboard with either pictures or sentences and then use the storyboard for story retells and summaries.

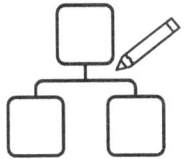

Notetaking & Graphic Organizers:

Fun Facts - Read or listen to the Background Information section of the book. Make a list of fun facts.

Venn Diagram – Compare and Contrast black bears and grizzlies.

Comprehension:

PAGES Strategy – Students learn an acronym to use while reading.

Comprehension Questions - Read or listen to the Background Information section and answer the open-ended questions either verbally or in writing. Practice answering in complete sentences by restating the question before providing an answer.

RACE Responses – Follow the directions to turn the short answers into complete RACE responses.

Paragraph & Essay Writing:

High Five Writing – Use the High Five template to brainstorm paragraphs based on writing prompts.

Compare/Contrast Essay - Use the I+P+P+C directions to construct a Compare & Contrast essay.

Create:

The highest level of Bloom's Taxonomy involves synthesizing what has been learned to create something new. This section contains a variety of creative writing prompts.

HOT Topics – Explore this section to learn how the activities described above fit into the 24 categories of Bloom's Revised Taxonomy.

Online Use

1. For online learning, mail the chapter book, *HANK THE TANK: ANIMAL IN THE SPOTLIGHT* to the student or use the e-book version of the chapter book and share it using Screen Share. Permission is granted for tele-education purposes. Email Activity Book pages to the school or home or upload pages onto Google Classroom. Activity pages may be printed wherever the student is located. A Purchaser's Password with directions to access printable versions of the Activity Pages may be found in the Downloads & Online Resources section near the end of the book.

2. Boom Cards may be used to play online games. Some Boom Cards are free, and some require an additional fee. The Word & Sentence Boom Cards contain the same sentences as those found in the Dictation section of the Activity Guide and may be used for reading practice.

3. Check all links to any online resources such as dice or Boom Cards to make sure they are still accessible and appropriate. Some sites such as YouTube contain ads and should be avoided or closely monitored depending on the setting.

4. You may display your PDFs for students using the SCREEN SHARE feature of Zoom. You may also display any pages of the Activity Book using a document camera. A cell phone may be used in place of a document camera. You may turn on the ANNOTATE feature of Zoom to type or write on the PDF to show students examples of how to construct written responses. It will not save as you scroll, but you may take a screenshot if desired. Students may use a variety of note-taking apps to write on the PDF on an iPad.

5. Via the SCREEN SHARE feature of Zoom, give students the ability to share their screen with you so you can see their written computer work. If they use pencil and paper, they may hold up their work or use a document camera to share it. They may also complete work in Google Classroom.

6. Online games including the virtual gameboard may be shared using SCREEN SHARE. Use caution if you give students REMOTE CONTROL access since they are basically taking over your screen. Some educators prefer the option of having students give them verbal directions while playing games. Never display your entire desktop using Screen Share.

7. If the student uses a Chrome Book, the Remote-Control feature will likely not be available on Zoom.

Gameboard Instructions

For 1-4 Players

The Hank Gameboard on the next page was designed to be used with a variety of cards and activities found throughout this resource. A printable color PDF is available in the Activity Pages PDF Download. Mix and match cards to create your own games. A FREE virtual version of the game is available at Boom Learning. Find a link to virtual dice on the website. Use caution when using YouTube as ads may pop up. If using virtual dice with Boom Cards, you will need to pull up both and toggle between the pages.

Directions:

1. Cut out the bears to be used as game pieces.
2. Players answer questions on cards, then roll the dice to see how many spaces they advance.
3. Players work together to pick up trash as they pass it and throw it in the trash can. Everyone is a winner!

GAMEBOARD – Color version available in PDF Downloads. Free digital version available at Boom Learning.

DECODING & ARTICULATION

INTRODUCTION

Articulation - Speech-language pathologists using this resource to work on speech-sound production at the word level may use the flashcards either in drills or in a Go Fish Game. Four-in-a-Row Games may also be used to work on sounds at the word level. To work on words in short sentences, read the items on the Dictation pages. To work on sounds in longer passages, students read the story poem.

DECODING:

Target Words - Have students practice reading words BEFORE and AFTER reading the story. Compare performance. Flash cards may be used for decoding practice. Make two sets of cards to play Go Fish or the Memory Game. Free Boom Cards are available that also contain these words. Sentences in the Dictation section may be used for reading practice.

Learned Words – Have students practice these using the Copy and Memory Strategy.

Four-in-a-Row – Students use a fun game format to practice finding words that contain ck, sh, th, ch, tch, wh, qu, nk, ng. A virtual version of this game is also available on Boom Cards for an additional fee.

Word Detective – After completing Game #4 of the Four-in-a-Row Game, students complete a word chart for the final /k/ and /ch/ endings. Use guided discovery to help students figure out the patterns and the spelling rules.

Calculate Accuracy: While the student reads each target word aloud, tally errors. The number of words per column appears below that column. Subtract 1 point if they make an error and don't self-correct. Subtract half a point for self-corrections, repetitions, or delays of more than 2 seconds. Add up Errors. Subtract this total from the total number of words per column. This is the Total Number Correct. Divide the Total Number Correct by the Total Number Per Column = % correct.

Target Words
from *Hank the Tank*
by Carolee Dean

Word List #1– Practice these words either by reading the lists below or using the flashcards on the following pages. The words with an asterisk * should be first introduced as LEARNED WORDS

Patterns	Words	Total
SINGLE CONSONANT		
n = /ng/ before /k/	blink, clank, clunk, drink, gunk, Hank, honk, junk, link, pink, prank, shrink, sink, tank, think, wink	/16
Consonant Digraphs & Trigraphs		
ng	bang, bing, clang, ding, gong, hang, long, length, ping, ring, sing, song, strength, string, thing, tong, wing, zing	/18
sh	she, shelf, shock, shrimp, shrink, bash, crash, dash, dish, fish, hush, smash, splash, stash, trash	/15
ch	chant, chap, check, chest, chip, chop, chunk, belch, bunch, French, hunch, lunch, much, munch, such	/15
tch	catch, hatch, hutch, snatch, stretch, ***watch**	/6

Target Words
from *Hank the Tank*
by Carolee Dean

Word List #2–Practice these words either by reading the lists below or using the flashcards on the following pages . The words with an asterisk * should be first introduced as LEARNED WORDS

Patterns	Words	Total
Digraphs (continued)		
ck	back, black, check, clack, crack, duck, hock, lick, quick, rack, sack, shock, smack, snack, stick, thick, track, trick, whack	/19
th (unvoiced)	Beth, broth, length, path, Seth, strength, thick, thin, thing, think, **three**, width, with	/13
th (voiced)	**the**, then, this	/3
Combinations		
wh	whack, **what**, whelk, whip, whisk	/5
qu	quest, quick, quit, squid	/4
Long/Naming Vowels		
Open Final Syllables	I, be, go, he, no, she, we	/7

Multi-Syllable Words

from *Hank the Tank*
by Carolee Dean

Word List #3–Practice these words either by reading the lists below or using the flashcards on the following pages . The words with an asterisk * should be first introduced as LEARNED WORDS

Patterns	Words	Total
Multi-Syllable Words	ban·dit, chic·ken, cul·prit, dump·ling, frost·ing, gum·bo, grub·bish, hid·den, ketch·up, kitch·en, man·go, mil·let, mus·sel, pol·lock, prob·lem, rac·ket, rub·bish, rot·ten, shal·lot, skil·let, sand·wich, totch·o	/22
-ing suffix words	bang·ing, bash·ing, bong·ing, clack·ing, clang·ing, clunk·ing, crash·ing, ding·ing, drink·ing, go·ing, hang·ing, honk·ing, pack·ing, shock·ing, shrink·ing, smack·ing, smash·ing, snatch·ing, splash·ing, stomp·ing	/20
Compound Words	chest·nut, chop·stick, drum·stick, gum·drop, him·**self**, shell·fish	/6
Stress on later syllable	a·**cross**, as·**sist**, at·**tract**, at·**tack**, con·**coct**, con·**fess** dis·**tress**·ing, *co-ex·**ist**, him·**self**, in·**vent**, sus·**pect**	/11

Learned Words

from *Hank the Tank*
by Carolee Dean

LEARNED WORDS – Ask students to read the Learned Words list below or use the flashcards. Make a list of words they do not easily recognize and teach them according to the Copy and Memorize procedure. These words are considered "Learned Words" because they must be "learned" by heart either because:

1) They do not follow regular spelling patterns.
2) They are regular but their patterns have not yet been introduced.

*Words that also appear on the target word lists

Learned Words (Irregular)	Learned Words (Not Yet Introduced)
any	*co-exist
are	for
do	have
does	or
doesn't	our
don't	*they
from	*three
of	too
one	*watch
to	*what
/10	/10

Names & Places

from *Hank the Tank*
by Carolee Dean

Names and Places – Study the names. Create a Vocabulary Foldable.

People and Places	Who or What Are They
Hank the Tank	A bear (or bears) in the Lake Tahoe area.
California	A state on the west coast.
Lake Tahoe	A mountain lake between Northern California and Nevada.
Tahoe Keys	A neighborhood along inland waterways in South Lake Tahoe.
The BEAR League	A wildlife rescue service.
Game Warden	An officer who protects people and animals and helps preserve plants, habitats, and ecosystems.

Word Cards

from *Hank the Tank*
by Carolee Dean

Flash Cards – Words on the following pages may be turned into flashcards by cutting them out and gluing them onto index cards OR you may use the card templates and copy them on cardstock before gluing. Make two copies to play card games like Go Fish or the Memory Game. Another option is to use the game board and have students read 5-10 words before rolling the dice. The flashcards are also available for FREE online as Boom Cards. Go to the Downloads & Online Resources section for details.

Go Fish – Make a deck of 52 cards by choosing 26 target words. Make two copies of each word and glue the words onto index cards or card stock.
1. Shuffle the cards.
2. Each player receives 7 cards.
3. The rest of the deck is placed face-down on the table.
4. During a turn, a player asks another player for a specific word in their hand. If the second player has the card, they must give it to the first player. That player places the pair face up in front of them and gets a second turn.
5. If the second player does not have that card, they say, "Go Fish," and the first player must choose a card from the deck.
6. The game is over when one player runs out of cards.
7. The winner is the person who has the most pairs of cards.

The Memory Game – Make a deck of 8 cards by choosing 4 target words. Make two copies of each word and glue the words onto index cards or card stock. (Note: Increase the number of cards in increments if the student can handle more cards). Some memory games are available on Boom Learning for a small additional fee.
1. Shuffle the cards and place them face down on the table.
2. Each player takes turns turning over 2 cards at a time and reading the words on the cards. If the cards match, the player gets to keep those cards. Do NOT rearrange the remaining cards.
3. The game ends when there are no cards left.
4. The winner is the person who has the most pairs of cards.

Card Template

Hank the Tank
Playing Cards

Hank the Tank
Playing Cards

Hank the Tank
Playing Cards

Hank the Tank
Playing Cards

Hank the Tank
Playing Cards

Hank the Tank
Playing Cards

Word Cards

from *Hank the Tank*
by Carolee Dean

blink	junk
clank	link
clunk	pink
drink	prank
gunk	shrink
Hank	sink
honk	tank

Word Cards

from *Hank the Tank*
by Carolee Dean

think	gong
wink	hang
NG	long
bang	length
bing	ping
clang	ring
ding	sing

Word Cards

from Hank the Tank
by Carolee Dean

song	**CK**
strength	back
string	black
thing	check
tong	clack
wing	crack
zing	duck

Word Cards

from *Hank the Tank*
by Carolee Dean

hock	snack
lick	stick
quick	stock
rack	thick
sack	track
shock	trick
smack	whack

Word Cards

from *Hank the Tank*
by Carolee Dean

SH

she

shelf

shock

shrimp

shrink

bash

crash

dash

dish

fish

hush

smash

splash

Word Cards

from *Hank the Tank*
by Carolee Dean

stash	chip
trash	chop
CH	chunk
chant	belch
chap	bunch
check	French
chest	hunch

Word Cards

from Hank the Tank
by Carolee Dean

lunch	hutch
much	snatch
munch	stretch
such	watch
TCH	**TH** voiced
catch	the
hatch	then

Word Cards

from *Hank the Tank*
by Carolee Dean

TH
voiceless

length

thick

path

thin

Seth

think

strength

thing

width

Beth

with

broth

Word Cards

from *Hank the Tank*
by Carolee Dean

QU

quest

quick

quit

squid

WH

whack

what

whelk

whip

whisk

Word Cards

from *Hank the Tank*
by Carolee Dean

Learned Words regular	too
for	watch
have	what
our	**Learned Words irregular**
or	any
they	are
three	do

Word Cards

from *Hank the Tank*
by Carolee Dean

does	**Compound Words**
doesn't	him·self
don't	chest·nut
from	chop·stick
of	drum·stick
one	gum·drop
to	shell·fish

Word Cards
from *Hank the Tank*
by Carolee Dean

Two-Syllable Words

grub·bish

ban·dit

hid·den

chick·en

ketch·up

cul·prit

kitch·en

dump·ling

man·go

frost·ing

mil·let

gum·bo

mus·sel

Word Cards

from *Hank the Tank*
by Carolee Dean

pol·lock	sand·wich
prob·lem	totch·o
rac·ket	**Suffix -ing**
rub·bish	bang**ing**
rot·ten	bash**ing**
shal·lot	bong**ing**
skil·let	clack**ing**

Word Cards

from Hank the Tank
by Carolee Dean

clang**ing**	honk**ing**
clunk**ing**	pack**ing**
crash**ing**	shock**ing**
ding**ing**	shrink**ing**
drink**ing**	smack**ing**
go**ing**	smash**ing**
hang**ing**	snatch**ing**

Word Cards

from *Hank the Tank*
by Carolee Dean

splash[ing]

stomp[ing]

2ⁿᵈ Syllable Stress

a·cross

as·sist

at·tract

at·tack

con·coct

con·fess

co-ex·ist

dis·tress

him·self

in·vent

sus·pect

FOUR-IN-A-ROW GAMES

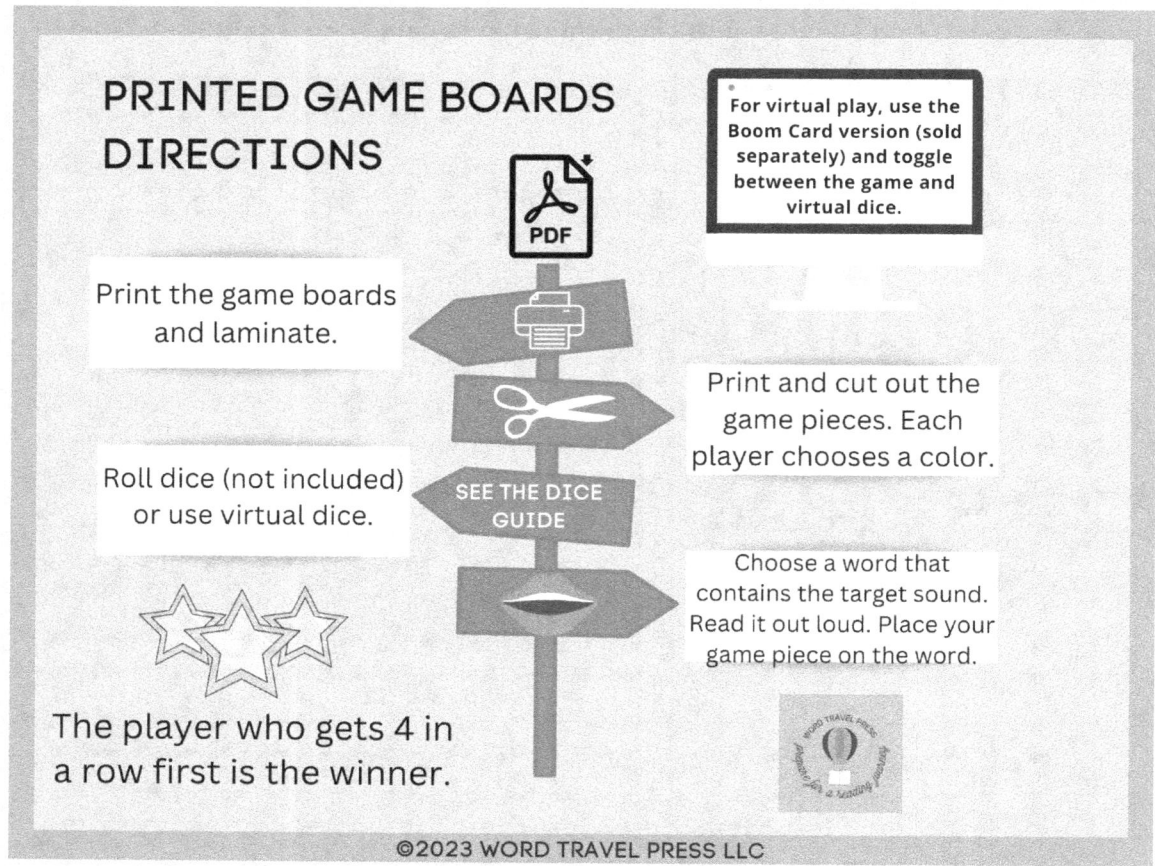

PRINTED GAME BOARDS
DIRECTIONS

For virtual play, use the Boom Card version (sold separately) and toggle between the game and virtual dice.

Print the game boards and laminate.

Print and cut out the game pieces. Each player chooses a color.

Roll dice (not included) or use virtual dice.

SEE THE DICE GUIDE

Choose a word that contains the target sound. Read it out loud. Place your game piece on the word.

The player who gets 4 in a row first is the winner.

©2023 WORD TRAVEL PRESS LLC

Game 1-Final Digraph and Trigraph Non-Words (1=sh, 2=th, 3=ck, 4= ch, 5= tch,6= ng)
Game 2-Initial Digraphs and Combinations (1= sh, 2 = ch, 3 = th, 4 = wh, 5 = qu, 6 = FREE)
Game 3- Final nk and ng (1=ang, 2 = ing, 3 = ong, 4 = ank, 5 = ink, 6 = unk
Game 4- Final /k/ (1=k, 2=c, 3=ck) and Final /ch/ (4=ch, 5=tch, 6= FREE)

After completing Game 4, have students organize words by sounds. Help them use guided learning to figure out the spelling patterns below:
K - comes after consonants (and double vowels which will be learned later)
C - comes after a closed (short) vowel in a two-or-more-syllable word.
CK – comes after a closed (short) vowel in a one-syllable word. Look at the CK word chart in the book to see if there are words that break this rule (note: compound words like flapjack do not follow this rule. Other rule breakers include pollock and attack).
CH – comes after consonants (and double vowels which will be learned later)
TCH – comes after a closed (short) vowel.

Download the PDF. Print. Cut out the game pieces.

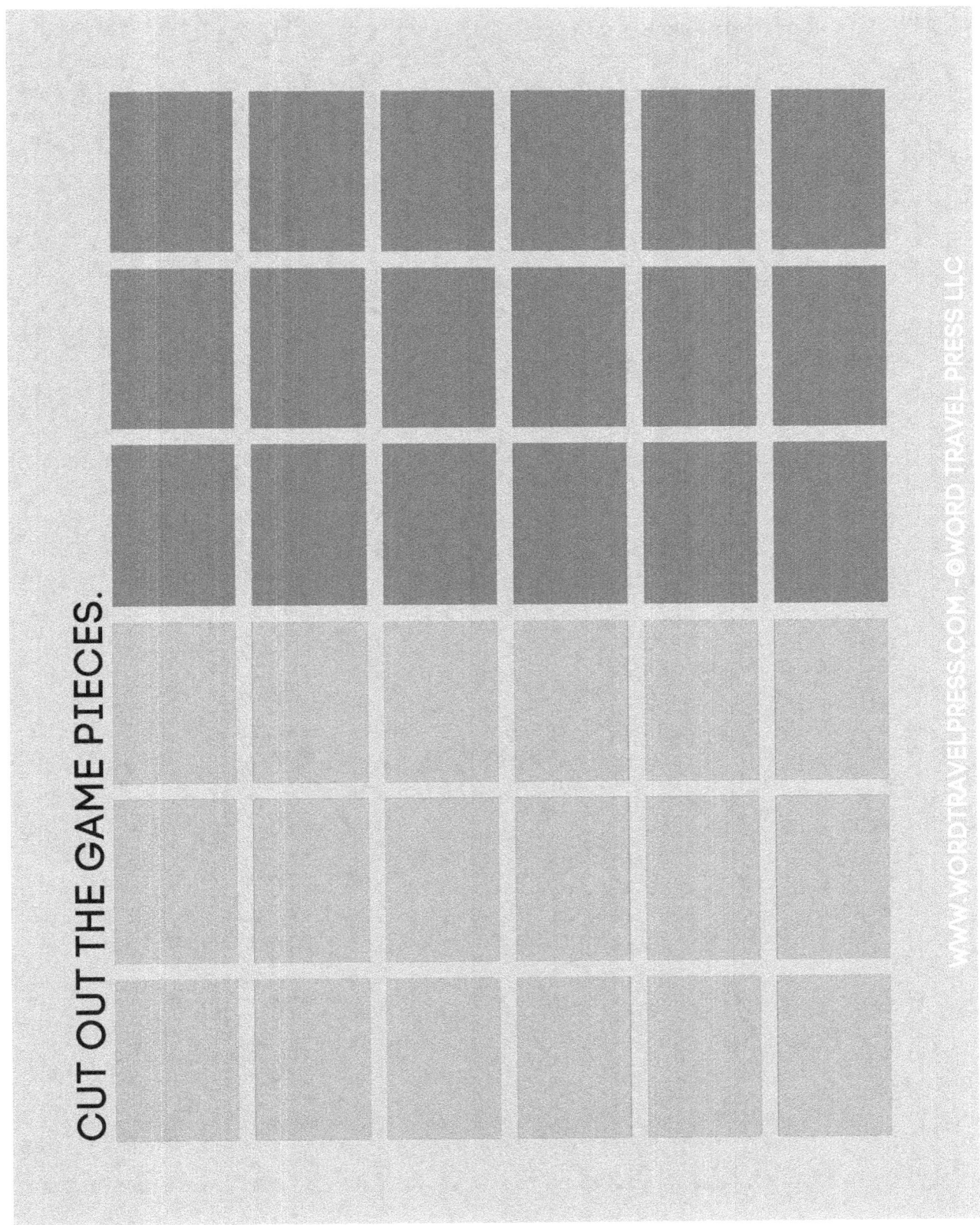

CUT OUT THE GAME PIECES.

Download the PDF. Print. Cut out the game pieces.

4 IN A ROW - FINAL SOUNDS (NON-WORDS)
1= SH, 2 = TH, 3 = CK, 4= CH, 5 = TCH, 6 = NG

	1	2	3	4	5	6
A	pish	duth	bock	felch	zatch	jung
B	zick	nesh	heth	ruck	gunch	detch
C	vitch	zung	fash	ving	gack	sanch
D	kang	tonch	votch	bosh	bith	leck
E	dilch	fong	lath	wutch	nush	joth

4 IN A ROW - INITIAL SOUNDS
1=SH, 2 = CH, 3 = TH, 4 = WH, 5 = QU, 6 = FREE

	1	2	3	4	5	6
A	she	chant	broth	whack	quest	shell
B	when	shelf	chap	path	what	quick
C	chip	quiz	shock	check	length	whelk
D	whip	Beth	squid	shrimp	chunk	width
E	with	quilt	whisk	quit	shrink	chest

4 IN A ROW - FINAL SOUNDS
1=ANG 2 = ING 3 = ONG 4 = ANK 5 = INK 6 = UNK

	1	2	3	4	5	6
A	bang	Hank	string	blink	gong	clunk
B	shrunk	clang	tank	ping	drink	long
C	song	gunk	hang	clank	ring	pink
D	bank	tong	junk	sang	prank	sing
E	pang	wing	strong	chunk	rang	plank

WWW.WORDTRAVELPRESS.COM - ©2023 WORD TRAVEL PRESS LLC

4 IN A ROW - FINAL SOUNDS
1= K, 2 = C, 3 = CK, 4= CH, 5 = TCH, 6 = FREE

	1	2	3	4	5	6
A	milk	picnic	back	belch	catch	junk
B	lick	pink	hectic	rack	lunch	hatch
C	hatch	munch	whisk	plastic	duck	hunch
D	mask	French	snatch	bulk	Atlantic	black
E	bunch	hitch	snack	stretch	hulk	frantic

Word Detective

based on *Hank the Tank*
by Carolee Dean

Directions: After completing GAME #4, write the words from the gameboard in the columns below that go with the final sound spelling. Can you discover the spelling rule by looking at what comes right before the final sound? Now add some words at the bottom that follow the same pattern. How many did you add?

K	C	CK	CH	TCH

PHONOLOGICAL AWARENESS

INTRODUCTION

Phonological Awareness is one of the foundational Components of Reading (COR). Learn more about this important skill on the COR INSTRUCTION page at https://wordtravelpress.com/.

Phonological awareness includes rhyming, counting syllables, and detecting initial, final, and medial sounds or phonemes. Prosody has also been included which involves recognizing the suprasegmental features of words such as rhythm, stress, pitch, and intonation.

Phonemic awareness is the part of phonological awareness that deals specifically with individual sounds. Students work with syllables and phonemes in the following activities by isolating, segmenting, adding, deleting, and substituting.

Phonemic skills are first taught as an oral skill (without letters) in the oral exercises found in the **Say It Again, Sam** activity. But phonemic awareness has the greatest impact when sounds are paired with letters and integrated with writing and spelling (Paulson, 2018 p. 234). In the **Sound Tracks** activity, students change one sound at a time to create new words. In **Rhyme Time** they work with the concepts of rhyme and alliteration with the added component of writing a sentence containing an alliteration. In **Feel the Beat**, students identify the stressed syllables in a line of poetry. In the **Dictation** activity, students draw upon their knowledge of sound-letter correspondences to write short sentences to dictation. The sentences in **Dictation** may also be used for reading practice.

Activities are described in more detail below:

Say It Again, Sam - Students work on deletion by repeating words and leaving out sounds or syllables. There are a total of 7 different activities. Students start by deleting part of a compound word. Then they delete a syllable from a two-syllable word. Then they delete the initial sounds, final sounds, and medial sounds. The medial sounds are parts of consonant blends. They are more difficult to isolate than single consonants. In this way, students move from more basic to more challenging phonological and phoneme awareness activities.

For a deeper and much more extensive exploration of phoneme awareness, see *Equipped for Reading Success: A Comprehensive, Step-By-Step Program for Developing Phonemic Awareness and Fluent Word Recognition* by David Kilpatrick.

See the following page for additional phonological awareness activities.

Continued

Feel the Beat, students draw a drumstick above the stressed syllables in lines of a poem. Then they read the poem by exaggerating the underlined words. They do this by saying the stressed syllables longer, louder, and with a slightly higher pitch. Finally, they read the poem with normal stress. Ask them if they can still feel the beat. If not, instruct them to try reading the poem like a robot, giving every word the same stress. Then read the poem again with stress on the highlighted syllables to bring out the difference.

In ***Rhyme Time #1,*** students circle words that rhyme and underline alliterations (words that start with the same sound). They then create a sentence that uses alliteration. This process also helps them understand and use literary devices. Additionally, switching between these three tasks requires students to use cognitive flexibility at both the letter-sound and meaning levels. Some students may not be ready for switching between tasks. For them, do one task at a time. For a metacognitive activity, ask students to think about how they tackle tasks. Would they rather complete all three steps for each target word before moving on OR would they prefer to do all the rhymes first, then all the alliterations, and then all the sentences? Get them talking about their internal processes and preferences.

In **Rhyme Time #2**, students fill in the blanks with words (or parts of two-syllable words) that fit the poem. Advanced students may be interested in a discussion of rhythm and meter. The excerpt on this page is written in trochaic tetrameter. Lines occasionally start with an added unstressed beat, but the overall rhythm is trochaic with the stress on the first syllable. Tetrameter refers to the fact that there are four sets or feet of trochee (the DUH-duh pattern):

Trochaic Tetrameter = DUH-duh, DUH-duh, DUH-duh, DUH-duh

In **Rhyme Time #3**, students create their own poems. This activity can be much more challenging than it appears, so students may benefit from working with partners. Complete an example poem as a class before asking students to tackle this activity on their own.

References:

Kilpatrick, D.A. (2016). Equipped for reading success: A comprehensive, step-by-step program for developing phonemic awareness and fluent word recognition. Syracuse, NY: Casey & Kirsch Publishers.

Paulson, L. H. (2018). Teaching phonemic awareness. In J.R. Birsh & S. Carreker (Eds.) *Multisensory teaching of basic language skills* (4th ed., pp. 205-253). Baltimore, MD: Paul H. Brookes Publishing Co.

Say It Again, Sam

Initial and Final Syllable Deletion
In Compound Words
based on *Hank the Tank*
by Carolee Dean

Directions: The teacher says a compound word. The student repeats. The teacher says which part to delete. The student says the part that is left.

Teacher	student	Teacher	Student
Say….		Say it again but leave out…	
		(initial syllable)	/5
chestnut	**chestnut**	chest	**nut**
chopstick	**chopstick**	chop	**stick**
drumstick	**drumstick**	drum	**stick**
gumdrop	**gumdrop**	gum	**drop**
shellfish	**shellfish**	shell	**fish**
		(final syllable)	/5
chestnut	**chestnut**	nut	**chest**
chopstick	**chopstick**	stick	**chop**
drumstick	**drumstick**	stick	**drum**
gumdrop	**gumdrop**	drop	**gum**
shellfish	**shellfish**	fish	**shell**

Say It Again, Sam
Two-Syllable Words

Initial Syllable Deletion
based on *Hank the Tank*
by Carolee Dean

Directions:
The teacher says a two-syllable word. The student repeats the word. The teacher says which syllable to delete. The student says the syllable that is left. Note that the stress in the initial word is on the second syllable.

Teacher	Student	Teacher	Student
Say….		Say it again but leave out…	
across	**across**	/uh/	**cross**
assist	**assist**	/uh/	**sist**
attract	**attract**	/uh/	**tract**
attack	**attack**	/uh/	**tack**
concoct	**concoct**	/kun/	**coct**
distress	**distress**	/dis/	**tress**
exist	**exist**	/ex/	**ist**
himself	**himself**	/him/	**self**
invent	**invent**	/in/	**vent**
suspect	**suspect**	/sus/	**pect**

/10

Say It Again, Sam
Two-Syllable Words

Final Syllable Deletion
based on *Hank the Tank*
by Carolee Dean

Directions:
The teacher says a two-syllable word. The student repeats the word. The teacher says which syllable to delete. The student says the syllable that is left. Note that the stress in the initial word is on the first syllable.

Teacher	student	Teacher	Student
Say....		Say it again but leave out...	
bandit	**bandit**	dit	**ban**
chicken	**chicken**	en	**chick**
culprit	**culprit**	prit	**cul**
dumpling	**dumpling**	ling	**dump**
frosting	**frosting**	ing	**frost**
gumbo	**gumbo**	bo	**gum**
ketchup	**ketchup**	up	**ketch**
kitchen	**kitchen**	en	**kitch**
mango	**mango**	go	**man(g)**
sandwich	**sandwich**	wich	**sand**

/10

Say It Again, Sam
One-Syllable Words

Initial Sound Deletion
based on *Hank the Tank*
by Carolee Dean

Directions: The teacher says the word. The student repeats the word. The teacher says which sound to delete. The student says what is left. Tell the student that some (but not all) will result in real words.

Teacher	Student	Teacher	Student
Say….		Say it again but leave out…	
think	**think**	/th/	**ink**
shelf	**shelf**	/sh/	**elf**
chant	**chant**	/ch/	**ant**
quit	**quit**	/kw/	**it**
chip	**chip**	/ch/	**ip**
song	**song**	/s/	**ong**
duck	**duck**	/d/	**uck**
whack	**whack**	/wh/	**ack**
Hank	**Hank**	/h/	**ank**
sink	**sink**	/s/	**ink**

/10

Say It Again, Sam
One-Syllable Words

Initial Sound Deletion in Blends
based on *Hank the Tank*
by Carolee Dean

Directions: The teacher says the word. The student repeats the word. The teacher says which sound to delete. The student says what is left.

Teacher	student	Teacher	Student
Say….		Say it again but leave out…	
bring	**bring**	/b/	**ring**
stick	**stick**	/s/	**tick**
crash	**crash**	/k/	**rash**
black	**black**	/b/	**lack**
snack	**snack**	/s/	**nack**
blink	**blink**	/b/	**link**
track	**track**	/t/	**rack**
smash	**smash**	/s/	**mash**
French	**French**	/f/	**rench**
squid	**squid**	/s/	**quid**

/10

Say It Again, Sam
One-Syllable Words

Final Sound Deletion
based on *Hank the Tank*
by Carolee Dean

Directions: The teacher says the word. The student repeats the word. The teacher says which sound to delete. The student says what is left. Some may be non-words.

Teacher	Student	Teacher	Student
Say….		Say it again but leave out…	
duck	**duck**	/k/	**duh**
shock	**shock**	/k/	**shaw**
shelf	**shelf**	/f/	**shell**
chest	**chest**	/t/	**chess**
bunch	**bunch**	/ch/	**bun**
shrink	**shrink**	/k/	**shrin/g/**
belch	**belch**	/ch/	**bell**
whelk	**whelk**	/k/	**whell**
quest	**quest**	/t/	**quess**
strength	**strength**	/th/	**streng**

/10

Medial Sound Deletion
based on *Hank the Tank*
by Carolee Dean

Directions: The teacher says the word. The student repeats the word. The teacher says which sound to delete. The student says what is left. Some may be non-words

Teacher	student	Teacher	Student
Say….		Say it again but leave out…	
string	string	/r/	sting
clank	clank	/l/	cank
crash	crash	/r/	cash
smash	smash	/m/	sash
splash	splash	/p/	slash
French	French	/r/	fench
snatch	snatch	/n/	satch
stick	stick	/t/	sick
chant	chant	/n/	chat
whisk	whisk	/s/	whick

/10

SOUND TRACKS

based on *Hank the Tank*
by Carolee Dean

Directions: For sound tracking, the teacher says the first word. The student repeats the word and uses the letters on page 62 to construct the word saying each sound. The student then reads the entire word. The teacher then says another word with one sound changed. The student says the new word, makes the sound change saying each sound, then reads the entire word. Some of the words may be non-words. Letters are also available for FREE on Boom Cards.

List 1 - NG	List 2 - NK	List 3 - SH	List 4 - CH
song	ink	ash	pinch
sung	sink	sash	punch
sing	slink	slash	lunch
sting	stink	splash	bunch
string	stank	spash	funch
tring	tank	pash	finch
bring	rank	pish	inch
ring	drank	ship	chin
rang	drink	shimp	chip
rung	rink	shrimp	chap
lung	hink	shrim	chop
slung	honk	shim	chomp
slang	hunk	sham	chom
sang	runk	mash	chum
tang	trunk	mush	chug

/45

SOUND TRACKS
based on *Hank the Tank*
by Carolee Dean

Directions: For sound tracking, the teacher says the first word. The student repeats the word and uses the letters on the next page to construct the word saying each sound. The student then reads the entire word. The teacher then says another word with one sound changed. The student says the new word, makes the sound change saying each sound, then reads the entire word. Some of the words may be non-words.

List 5 – TH	List 6 – WH,QU	List 7 - CK	List 8 - TCH
bath	quit	lick	itch
path	quid	lack	hitch
pith	squid	slack	pitch
with	squad	stack	patch
bith	quad	tack	satch
nith	quap	track	snatch
thin	quip	trick	natch
thit	whip	truck	notch
thet	whis	ruck	nutch
theft	whisk	rock	lutch
thef	whist	lock	clutch
thaf	whit	clock	cletch
tham	whim	clack	fletch
math	wham	lack	fetch
moth	whum	luck	etch

/45

SOUND TRACKS
based on *Hank the Tank*
by Carolee Dean

Directions: For sound tracking, the teacher says the first word. The student repeats the word and uses the letters on the next page to construct the word saying each sound. The student then reads the entire word. The teacher then says another word with one sound changed. The student says the new word, makes the sound change saying each sound, then reads the entire word. Some of the words may be non-words.

List 8 - Mix	List 10 - Mix	List 11 - Mix	List 12 - Mix
ash	rack	amp	sing
rash	track	champ	sting
trash	trash	chimp	string
track	trush	chip	strung
tack	tush	chin	stung
stack	shut	inch	sung
stuck	shat	pinch	sing
struck	chat	punch	thing
truck	that	bunch	thick
trick	than	bun	thin
tick	can	ban	shin
chick	catch	bash	shim
pick	hatch	bish	sham
pit	hutch	pish	mash
tip	hitch	ship	match

SOUND TRACKS
Letters
based on *Hank the Tank*
by Carolee Dean

Directions: Cut out the letters below to use for the Sound Tracks Activity. Enlarge as needed and glue them onto card stock to make them easier to pick up. A digital version of the activity may be found for FREE at Boom Learning.

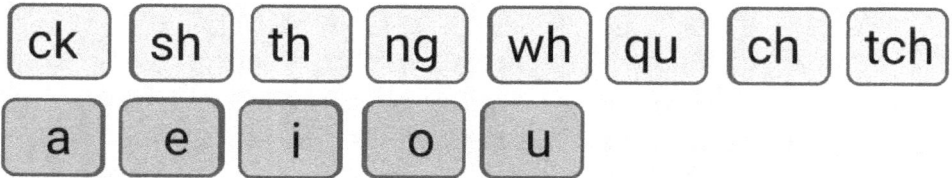

ck	sh	th	ng	wh	qu	ch	tch

a	e	i	o	u

b	c	d	f	g	h	j	k	l	m

n	p	r	s	t	v	w	x	y	z

 # DICTATION

CK Words

based on *Hank the Tank*
by Carolee Dean

Directions: The following sentences may be used for dictation, spelling, articulation, and/or reading practice.

Word	Sentence
1. back	Pat went back to the van.
2. black	Is that cub black?
3. duck	The duck swam in the pond.
4. lick	Did Bill lick the pan?
5. rack	Is the cup on the rack?
6. sack	The sack has nibs in it.
7. track	Do not track in mud.
8. smack	Did Sam smack his lips?
9. snack	Let us get a snack.
10. stick	Dad has a stick of gum.

/10

DICTATION

NG & NK Words

based on *Hank the Tank*
by Carolee Dean

Directions: The following sentences may be used for dictation, spelling, articulation, and/or reading practice.

Word	Sentence
1. bang	Did Rex bang on the glass?
2. long	The path was long.
3. ring	Jen got a ring as a gift.
4. wing	Can the vet fix the wing?
5. string	Get the black string.
6. drink	The red drink is hot.
7. junk	Will Max pick up that junk?
8. pink	Jill just got a pink dress.
9. prank	Is this a prank?
10. sink	Ben set the cup in the sink.

/10

DICTATION

SH Words

based on *Hank the Tank*
by Carolee Dean

Directions: The following sentences may be used for dictation, spelling, articulation, and/or reading practice.

Word	Sentence
1. shelf	1. Sam set the pan on the shelf.
2. shock	2. It was a big shock.
3. shrimp	3. Pam had shrimp and grits.
4. shrink	4. Did the pants shrink?
5. dash	5. I will dash to the hut.
6. dish	6. The ham is in the dish.
7. fish	7. The fish is not hot.
8. trash	8. Did Bob spill the trash?
9. stash	9. Will Ed stash the cans?
10. smash	10. Did Ted smash the glass?

/10

DICTATION

FINAL /CH/ WORDS

based on *Hank the Tank*
by Carolee Dean

Directions: The following sentences may be used for dictation, spelling, articulation, and/or reading practice.

Word	Sentence
1. bunch	Fred had a bunch of nuts.
2. catch	Did Brad catch the dog?
3. hatch	Did the eggs hatch?
4. lunch	When is lunch?
5. snatch	Will Fran snatch the traps?
6. French	Greg had a French dip.
7. munch	The kids will munch on crust.
8. hunch	I have a hunch Stan is back.
9. belch	Did Cliff just belch?
10. stretch	I must stretch my legs.

/10

DICTATION

TH Words

based on *Hank the Tank*
by Carolee Dean

Directions: The following sentences may be used for dictation, spelling, articulation, and/or reading practice.

Word	Sentence
1. thick	That milk is thick.
2. thin	Is the crust thin?
3. think	I think I will go to camp.
4. thing	That thing is big.
5. broth	The broth has red stuff in it.
6. length	The length of that log is an inch.
7. path	We must stick to the path.
8. with	Will Max get ham with that?
9. Seth	Did Seth get the dog dish?
10. Beth	Will Beth scrub the grill?

/10

DICTATION

WH & QU Words

based on *Hank the Tank*
by Carolee Dean

Directions: The following sentences may be used for dictation, spelling, articulation, and/or reading practice.

Word	Sentence
1. quest	Tess is on a quest.
2. quick	The cub is not quick.
3. quit	Bill must quit this task.
4. squid	Is a squid a fish?
5. whack	Ross will whack the rug.
6. what	What is the next step?
7. whelk	Is a whelk a clam?
8. whip	Mom will whip up a bit of grub.
9. whisk	Did Bess get the whisk?
10. when	When will Jill get back?

/10

Feel the Beat
based on *Hank the Tank*
by Carolee Dean

Directions: Read the lines of poetry below.
1. Draw a drumstick above each stressed beat. Follow the pattern in the first line.
2. Read the poem and tap the stressed words with a pencil or drumstick.
3. Read the lines of poetry again, but this time in your normal voice.
4. Can you still feel the beat?

Excerpt from *Hank the Tank* (Level 2 – The HOT ROD series)

Hank is back quick as a wink,

splash·ing in the kitch·en sink.

He hits the hutch. Don't smash that shelf!

Hank the Tank just helps himself.

Soft drinks, flap·jacks, man·go whips.

Watch it go·ing to his hips.

Whelk, that smells a bit like clams.

Thick crust, thin crust, soft plump hams.

Feel the Beat
based on *Hank the Tank*
by Carolee Dean

ANSWERS

Excerpt from *Hank the Tank* (Set 2, Book 1 – The HOT ROD series)

Hank is back quick as a wink,

splash·ing in the kitch·en sink.

He hits the hutch. Don't smash that shelf!

Hank the Tank just helps him·self.

Soft drinks, flap·jacks, man·go whips.

Watch it go·ing to his hips.

Whelk, that smells a bit like clams.

Thick crust, thin crust, soft plump hams.

Rhyme Time #1
based on *Hank the Tank*
by Carolee Dean

Directions: Read the target words below, and then:
1. Circle words that rhyme - end with the same vowel + consonant(s).
2. Underline words that start with the same sound. This is called *alliteration.*
3. Use the target word and a word that starts with the same sound to write a sentence. Use another piece of paper if needed.

1. Hank (tank)   hash   thick   (bank)   had

Sentence: Hank had hash for lunch.

2. trash   smack   smash   track   crash   trap

Sentence:

3. hunch   hug   lunch   hunk   lunch   fill

Sentence:

4. crack   crab   stack   crash   spat   back

Sentence:

5. think   drop   pink   thick   drink   thin

Sentence:

6. quit   win   quest   quick   grit   sit

Sentence:

7. catch   hatch   can   hat   cash   snatch

Sentence:

8. whack   shack   whip   sack   when   track

Sentence:

Rhyme Time #1
based on *Hank the Tank*
by Carolee Dean

ANSWERS

Sentence content will vary

Rhymes - 15, Alliterations – 15 = 30 Total

1. Hank   (tank)   hash   thick   (bank)   <u>had</u>

2. trash   smack   (smash)   <u>track</u>   (crash)   <u>trap</u>

3. hunch   <u>hug</u>   (lunch)   hunk   (bunch)   fill

4. crack   crab   (stack)   <u>crash</u>   spat   (back)

5. think   drop   (pink)   thick   (drink)   <u>thin</u>

6. quit   win   <u>quest</u>   <u>quick</u>   (grit)   (sit)

7. catch   (hatch)   <u>can</u>   hat   <u>cash</u>   (snatch)

8. whack   (shack)   <u>whip</u>   (sack)   <u>when</u>   (track)

Rhyme Time #2

based on *Hank the Tank*
by Carolee Dean

Directions:
1. Write words in blank boxes to complete the poem.
2. For two-syllable words, use two boxes.
3. Read the finished poem out loud.
4. Use the eraser end of your pencil to tap the words that have drumsticks, These are stressed syllables.

| The | / | ing | | / | | | / | had | a | / | snack. |

| I | hope | / | he | won't | / | be | | / | ing | back. | / |

| The | | / | | chil | dren | / | | and | / | hid |

| / | as | the | / | | | / | a | lid. | / |

Example:.
The **stink**-ing **ban-dit** had a snack.
I hope he won't be **slink**-ing back.
The **fran-tic** chil-dren **ran** and hid
as the **cul-prit bit** a lid.

Rhyme Time #3
based on *Hank the Tank*
by Carolee Dean

Directions:
1. Write a pair of words that rhyme with each other in the A boxes.
2. Write a different pair of words that rhyme with each other in the B boxes.
3. Write words in the rest of the empty boxes to make a poem.
4. For two-syllable words, use two boxes.
5. Read the finished poem out loud.
6. Use the eraser end of your pencil to tap the words that have drumsticks. These are stressed syllables.

Rhyme Pair Examples: can, pan; thick, trick; trash, dash; sink, think; dish, fish; munch, lunch; sing, thing; chip, sip

A

A

B

B

Cognitive Flexibility

INTRODUCTION

What is Cognitive Flexibility
Cognitive flexibility impacts reading, writing, spelling, and more. It is an important executive function skill that centers on the ability to switch between different types of information. It can involve switching between different tasks or thinking about more than one concept at a time. Working memory is an important element of cognitive flexibility that helps a person manage more than one task, concept, or piece of information at the same time.

How Cognitive Flexibility Impacts Reading
Specific to reading, cognitive flexibility is essential for both decoding and comprehension. Students need cognitive flexibility to be able to hold different possible pronunciations for a letter or combination of letters in mind while decoding unfamiliar words. At the same time, they must consider the word's meaning. Working memory enables a reader to compare the possible pronunciations of a word with words in their lexicon (internal dictionary). While they are figuring out how to pronounce the word and determining what the word means, a reader must also hold the rest of the sentence in mind. The content and structure of the sentence will also affect the meaning of the word. If a word has multiple meanings, cognitive flexibility is required to hold the possible options in short-term memory while making judgments about the best fit within the context of the sentence and paragraph. While there are many tasks that are useful for developing cognitive flexibility, there are not many that directly relate to reading and decoding. The activity on the next page was designed to address executive function skills that directly relate to a structured literacy scope and sequence. By sorting words that belong to two different categories simultaneously, students can work on cognitive flexibility.

Cognitive Flexibility Game

The target words in the FREE online Boom game are: dash, shallot, crash, splash, shrimp, catfish, sandwich, chicken, chant, munch, chips, belch

This activity Boom Deck has three component parts:
1. First students sort words into two categories: Foods & Actions
1. Next, they sort the SAME cards into two different categories: SH & CH
3. Finally, they sort the same words on a 2x2 matrix while considering all 4 categories at once.

Go to page 156 of this Activity Book for information about how to access Boom Card resources.

For additional information about Cognitive Flexibility as well as a FREE printable activity based on Level 1 of the HOT ROD series (CVC, CCVC, CVCC, CCCVC, etc), visit the Cognitive Flexibility Page at www.wordtravelpress.com.

References:
Cartwright, K.B. (2023). *Executive skills and reading comprehension: A guide for educators* (Second Edition). New York, NY: Guildford Press.

Tunmer, W.E., & Chapman, J.W. (2012). Does set for variability mediate the influence of vocabulary knowledge on the development of word recognition skills? *Scientific Studies of Reading*, 16(2), 122-140.

Vadasy, P.F., Sanders, E.A., Cartwright, K.B. (2022). Cognitive flexibility in beginning decoding and encoding. *The Journal of Education for Students Placed at Risk*, in press.

Zipke, M. (2016). The importance of flexibility of pronunciation in learning to decode: A training study in set for variability. *First Language*. 36 (1), 71-86.

Cognitive Flexibility
& Other Executive Functions

The two category sorts appear on the next two pages as well as on the Boom Card Game. Students start with those activities to prepare for the Multiple Classification Activity which is below. That activity is only available on Boom Cards, but it is free. It has 8 tasks like the one shown here. You will need a Boom Learning account to play the game. You may sign up for a free Boom Account at www.wow.boomlearning.com

Below is a sample of the Multiple Classification Task. Observe that there are two ACTIONS and one FOOD. Therefore, a FOOD is needed for B1.

There are two SH words and one CH word, therefore a CH word is needed for B1.

B1 must be a FOOD that contains CH. There are three possible answers.

Drag the correct word into the empty box. Say the words out loud.

	1	2
A	munch	splash
B		shrimp

dash	chips	shallot
chant	crash	chicken
belch	sandwich	catfish

Answers: *chips, chicken, sandwich.*

Cognitive Flexibility
Category Sort for CH and SH

Directions: Cut out the words and glue them into the correct category.

sandwich	chips	splash	shallot
belch	chicken	dash	crash
shrimp	catfish	munch	chant

SH   **CH**

Cognitive Flexibility
Category Sort for FOODS & ACTIONS

Directions: Cut out the words and glue them into the correct category.

sandwich	chips	splash	shallot
belch	chicken	dash	crash
shrimp	catfish	munch	chant

FOODS   ACTIONS

MORPHOLOGY

INTRODUCTION

While phonemes represent the smallest unit of sound, morphemes represent the smallest unit of meaning. English is a morphophonemic language which means that the phonemes and the morphological structure work together to affect how words are pronounced. Read more about this important skill at the COR Instruction page of the website.

Morpho Mania #1: -ING is a suffix that means *happening in the present,* but just because a word ends in ING does not mean it is acting like a verb with a suffix. Box off ING and then see if what is left is a baseword. That is one way to tell if ING is acting like a suffix. This activity helps students determine when –ING is acting like a suffix and when it is just part of a word. You may want to do the Sentence Mania activity in the Sentence section directly after this activity to further explore the ING concept.

Morpho Mania #2: Re- is a Latin prefix meaning *again, back,* or *backward*
Students study the words and their meanings. Then they make cards for the Morpho Mania Memory Game. You may use the print version to make your own game cards or go to BOOM Learning to find a digital version for an additional fee.

Morpho Mania #3: Students will explore the Latin root – *tract* (to pull, draw, drag, or move). Go over the words and definitions with students and then have them read the book or listen to the Background Information to tally how many times they hear words containing this root. You may make cards for the Morpho Mania Memory Game which are also available for a small additional fee at Boom Learning.

Morpho Mania #4 – Students explore the etymology of the word, bear. Then they use terms to write a paragraph.

Students with dyslexia may continue to need these words and definitions read aloud to them as they play the matching game. That's okay. Exposure to the concepts helps build vocabulary. It also connects to concepts in the decodable book, *Hank the Tank*. Read the section in the book about "Dogs and Bears" to find several examples of *tract* in words like *distract, retractable,* and *attract.*
Reference:

Farrell, L.M., & Cushen-Whte, N. (2018). Structured literacy instruction . In J.R. Birsh & S. Carreker (Eds.) *Multisensory teaching of basic language skills* (4th ed., pp. 35-72). Baltimore, MD: Paul H. Brookes Publishing Co.

Morpho Mania #1
Suffix *-ing*
based on *Hank the Tank*
by Carolee Dean

-ING is a suffix that means *happening in the present,* but just because a word ends in ING does not mean it is acting like a suffix. Box off ING and then see if what is left is a baseword. Circle Yes if –ING is acting like a suffix.

Word	Baseword	-ING Suffix	
r[i n g]	ring	Yes	(No)
r i n g[i n g]	ring	(Yes)	No
s i n g		Yes	No
s i n g i n g		Yes	No
s n a t c h i n g		Yes	No
g o i n g		Yes	No
s t r i n g		Yes	No
s h o c k i n g		Yes.	No
w i n g		Yes.	No
s n a c k i n g		Yes	No
h o n k i n g		Yes	No
c a t c h i n g		Yes	No

Morpho Mania #1
Suffix -*ing*
based on *Hank the Tank*
by Carolee Dean

ANSWERS

Word	Baseword	-ING Suffix
r i n g	ring	Yes **(No)**
r i n g i n g	ring	**(Yes)** No
s i n g	sing	Yes **(No)**
s i n g i n g	sing	**(Yes)** No
s n a t c h i n g	snatch	**(Yes)** No
g o i n g	go	**(Yes)** No
s t r i n g	string	Yes **(No)**
s h o c k i n g	shock	**(Yes)** No
w i n g	wing	Yes **(No)**
s n a c k i n g	snack	**(Yes)** No
h o n k i n g	honk	**(Yes)** No
c a t c h i n g	catch	**(Yes)** No

Morpho Mania #2
Prefix *re-*
based on *Hank the Tank*
by Carolee Dean

Re: Latin prefix meaning **again, back,** or **backward**

Directions: Study the words and their meanings. Then make cards for the Morpho Mania Memory Game.

Word	Meaning
react	To act **back** or act in response to something. Ex: How did she <u>react</u> to the news?
release	To loosen **back**, stretch out, let go. Ex. He <u>released</u> the dog from the cage.
relocate	To locate something **again** by putting it in a different location. Ex. Our family <u>relocated</u> to Denver.
remember	To bring **back** to memory. Ex. I <u>remember</u> our trip to the mountains.
remove	To move **back** or take away. Ex. Please <u>remove</u> the trash from the yard.
replace	To fill a place **again** with something else. Ex. We <u>replaced</u> the old clock with a new one.
report	To carry or bring **back** news or information. Ex. I wrote a <u>report</u> about black bears.
respect	To see **again** with special consideration. Ex. I have a lot of <u>respect</u> for people who work with animals.

Morpho Mania #3
Root *tract*

based on *Hank the Tank*
by Carolee Dean

Tract: Latin/Greek stem meaning **drag, pull,** or **draw toward**

Directions: Study the words and their meanings. Then reread the section on "Dogs and Bears" and the section on "Can Bears and Humans Co-exist" from *Hank the Tank.* Make a tally of how many times you find each word.

Word	Meaning
retract	To **pull** or take something back. Ex. The newspaper had to <u>retract</u> a comment that was not accurate.
retractable	Able to be **pulled** back. Ex. A <u>retractable</u> leash can be dangerous if you are not able to pull your dog away from danger quickly.
distract	To **pull** someone away from something. Ex. Please do not <u>distract</u> me from my work.
attract	To **draw** or **pull** an object, person, or animal toward something. Ex. The rotten fruit <u>attracted</u> the bears to their yard.
attractant	A thing that **draws** or **pulls** an object, person, or animal toward itself. Ex. Dog food that is left outside can be a powerful <u>attractant</u> to a hungry bear.

Tally how many times you find the words below:

retract:

retractable:

distract:

attract:

attractant:

Morpho Mania
Memory Game
RE

Memory Game Cards – Cut out the cards, paste onto construction paper, turn upside down, and shuffle to play the memory game. Each player turns over two cards at a time to match the words to their meanings. They are also available as BOOM cards.

react	report	To bring back to memory.
release	respect	To take away.
relocate	retract	To fill a place with something else.
remember	To act in response to something.	To bring back news or information.
remove	To let go.	To see again with special consideration.
replace	To put something in a different location.	To pull or take something back.

Morpho Mania
Memory Game
Tract

Memory Game Cards – Cut out the cards, paste onto construction paper, turn upside down, and shuffle to play the memory game. Each player turns over two cards at a time to match the words to their meanings. They are also available as BOOM cards.

retract	distract	To pull something away from something.
attractant	attract	To draw or pull an object, person, or animal toward something.
retractable	Able to be pulled back.	A thing that draws or pulls an object, person, or animal toward itself.
tractor	To pull or take something back.	A machine that pulls.

Morpho Mania #4
Bear Etymology
by Carolee Dean

How The Bear Got Its Name

Etymology is the history of language. It's interesting to learn about the history of words, where they came from, and how they have changed. *Ursa* is the Latin word for bear while *arktos* is the Greek word. *Ursidae* is the scientific name for animals in the bear family.

Hunters who lived in the north had a taboo against saying the name of certain animals. This taboo may have been because they were afraid that if they used the animal's name, they would call it and it might attack them. They may have worried about scaring away an animal they were hunting. It is believed that the original terms *ursa* and *arktos* were replaced for this reason with The old German root word, *bero*, meaning "brown one." The Dutch words are *beer* and *bruin*. These words come from the PIE (Proto-Indo-European) root *bher* which means bright or brown.
See etymonline.com for more information.

The Constellations

Ursa Major means "greater bear" in Latin while "Ursa Minor" means the "lesser bear." They are constellations in the northern sky that are sometimes called the Big Dipper and the Little Dipper because they are shaped like ladles. Polaris, The North Star, is one of the stars in Ursa Minor. The North Star or Pole Star moves only very slightly. For that reason, sailors have used it throughout the ages to help guide them because it represents true north. Many cultures have stories about the origin of the North Star.

The Greek Myth

There is a story from Greek Mythology about how the two bears ended up in the sky. Callisto was a nymph who had a child named Arcas with Zeus, the king of the Greek gods. His wife, Hera, was very jealous. To protect Callisto and her son, Zeus turned them into bears and placed them in the night sky.

The Football Team

UCLA is a university in Southern California. The grizzly bear is the bear on the California state flag. The UCLA football team used to be called the Grizzlies. When the university joined the Pacific Coast Conference, that name was already being used by another team in the Conference. That was when they changed their name to the Bruins. http://www.espn.com/magazine.

Morpho Mania #4
Bear Etymology
(continued)
based on *Hank the Tank*
by Carolee Dean

Arctic – Of the north.
Bruin – A bear. The name of the UCLA football team.
Ursa Major – The greater bear. A constellation in the north.
Ursa Minor – The lesser bear. A constellation in the north. One of its stars is Polaris.
Polaris – The North Star
Polar Bear – A bear that lives in the north.

Directions: Read about the etymology of the word, *bear*, on the previous page. Use as many of the terms above to write an original paragraph or story about a bear. Write on the back or use additional paper if needed.

_____

_____

_____

_____

_____

_____

_____

_____

VOCABULARY

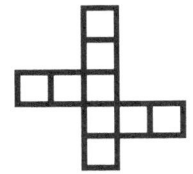

INTRODUCTION

Vocabulary is a foundational building block of both listening and reading comprehension, but it can be challenging to include robust vocabulary when focusing on limited constructs such as closed syllable types. On the other hand, even these most basic word forms can provide opportunities for exploring advanced vocabulary when multi-syllable words are included. When vocabulary is content-rich and comes from material related to the curriculum, repeated exposure to words is more natural. Read about vocabulary on the page for COR Instruction on the website.

The stories in Level 1 of the HOT ROD series had words divided into syllables. In Level 2, it is assumed that students have learned to divide words with a VC/CV pattern, so only words NOT following this pattern have been divided in the story. For those still struggling with dividing syllables, all multi-syllable words on the flashcards have been divided. However, the vocabulary lists do NOT divide words. It can be helpful to have students place a / between syllables if needed in the chapter book.

Pre-teach new words before students are asked to read them in context. It can also be helpful to teach students strategies for determining the meaning of new words on their own by looking at the context **before** they are told the definition. Students with dyslexia need even more exposure to a word than their peers, so if they have already been introduced to a word, it is still helpful to explore the **Word Clues** activities. Context is crucial to understanding multiple-meaning words.

Rereading helps students develop confidence and fluency, but there needs to be a meaningful reason for rereading a text. Many of the activities included here require a student to reread words during a game or while searching for a definition. In addition, the Scavenger Hunts require a student to go back through the story in the chapter book looking for specific words.

References:
Wright, T.S., & Neuman, S.B. (2015). The power of content-rich vocabulary instruction. *Perspectives on Language and Literacy*, 41 (3), 25-28.

Shanahan, T. (2015). Are you lactating? On the importance of academic language. *Perspectives on Language and Literacy, 41*(3), 14-16.

ACTIVITIES

Word Clues – There are three levels of activities to help students develop the skills needed to use context clues to determine the meaning of a word.

Level 1 – Seek and Find: Sometimes the meaning of a new word is stated directly within the context of a nearby sentence. In this activity, students simply underline the definition that is provided.

Level 2 – Making Inferences: Sometimes hints about a word's meaning are given, but the meaning is not stated outright. For this reason, students are also asked to write down what they think the word means based on the clues.

Level 3 – Opposite Meanings: Sometimes the context tells us the opposite of what a word means. Look for negative words like **no, don't, instead**, or **unfortunately** as a clue that the information may be hinting at the opposite meaning. Then write down what you think the word really means.

Just for Fun – Snack Attack Word Mash-Up: Sometimes the word itself will contain hints about it's meaning. This is especially true for food combinations. Students will enjoy making a few new food combinations of their own.

Scavenger Hunt – Follow the directions to search through the rhyming story to find specific words. Use those words to discover a secret message.

Multiple Meaning Match Up – Students match words in a memory game as they explore double meanings.

Idioms – Students make a vocabulary foldable to explore figurative language.

Wonder of Words
The two word lists below may be used for a variety of activities and games listed on the next page.

WOW (Wonder of Words) Vocabulary #1 is comprised of target words from the story, *Hank the Tank*. Even short words or words with multiple meanings may be unfamiliar to some students and will present an opportunity to learn new word meanings.

WOW (Wonder of Words) Vocabulary #2 is from the Background Information section and is significantly more challenging. Students with dyslexia may need these words and definitions read aloud for them. Allow any student who needs it to have the list of words from the book available while completing activities.

WOW VOCABULARY CARD OPTIONS

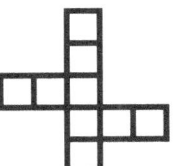

Choose One

1. **Alphabet** – Cut out the words and put them in alphabetical order. Then use the word list to check for accuracy.

2. **Vocabulary Foldable** – Follow the directions to complete a vocabulary foldable.

3. **Memory Game** – Make two copies of the words. Glue them onto construction paper and play the memory game by turning the cards face down. Pick two at a time, looking for a match. Read the words out loud as you turn them over. Start with 5 sets of words. When that is manageable, go up to 6, then 7, then 8 or more.

4. **Go Fish –** Fish are much healthier to eat than trash. Go through the vocabulary cards and cut out the ones that are healthy foods. There are blank cards that you can use to add a few of your own. Make two sets of cards. Play Go Fish by shuffling the cards and passing them out. Each player gets 5 cards. The rest of the cards are placed face-down on the table in a pile. Players take turns asking other players if they have a certain card that matches a card they already have. If the player has that card, they must give it up. The person who received it then places both cards face up on the table and gets another turn. If the player does NOT have that card, they say, "Go Fish," and the person who requested it must pick a card from the pile. When all the cards have been played, the player with the most cards wins.

Word Clues #1
Seek and Find
based on *Hank the Tank*
by Carolee Dean

DIRECTIONS: Read the word in the left column. Find it in the sentence and circle it. Then underline the information that helps you understand the meaning of the word.

Word	Sentences
moniker	Authorities say that "Hank" was a moniker, a nickname, given by the public to three different bears.
chest blaze	Some bears have chest blazes, white markings, in the shape of stars or other patterns.
culvert traps	Officers set up culvert traps. These are traps that resemble the culverts used for storm drainage.
haze	The last step is to "haze" the animal. They open the door to let the bear out of the trap. As they release it, they make loud, annoying sounds. They might also shoot bean bags at the bear or use a Taser.
hyperphagia	Late summer is when bears go into hyperphagia in Tahoe. They binge eat everything they can find to build up fat reserves. Sometimes they double their body weight.
attractant	Most bear break-ins are due to people not keeping attractants away from bears. Attractants are things like barbecue grills with grease left on them and trash not kept in a secure container.
scavenger	Black bears are scavengers, which means they will eat dead organic matter like rotting fruit that has fallen from trees.

Word Clues #1
Seek and Find

ANSWERS

Word	Sentences
moniker	Authorities say that "Hank" was a moniker, a nickname, given by the public to three different bears.
chest blaze	Some bears have chest blazes white markings, in the shape of stars or other patterns.
culvert traps	Officers set up culvert traps. These are traps that resemble the culverts used for storm drainage.
haze	The last step is to "haze" the animal. They open the door to let the bear out of the trap. As they release it, they make loud, annoying sounds. They might also shoot bean bags at the bear or use a Taser.
hyperphagia	Late summer is when bears go into hyperphagia in Tahoe. They binge eat everything they can find to build up fat reserves. Sometimes they double their body weight.
attractant	Most bear break-ins are due to people not keeping attractants away from bears. Attractants are things like barbecue grills with grease left on them and trash not kept in a secure container.
scavenger	Black bears are scavengers, which means they will eat dead organic matter like rotting fruit that has fallen from trees.

Word Clues #2
Making Inferences
based on *Hank the Tank*
by Carolee Dean

DIRECTIONS: Circle the target word in the sentence. Underline the hints that help you understand the meaning. Write down what you think the meaning is based on the hints.

Word	Sentences
canid	Bears have developed a fear of canids. A barking, snarling dog looks just as dangerous to a mother bear as a wolf or coyote.
meaning	
co-exist	Most people who live in bear country feel that if humans were more careful, they could peacefully co-exist with bears. Although most residents have learned to live in harmony with bears and even consider them their neighbors, more and more people are moving into bear country from the city.
meaning	
retract	You can retract the lead and pull it back in by pushing a button, but it isn't easy in an emergency to do this quickly.
meaning	
habitat	Bear habitats are shrinking because humans are moving into them. When we get upset about bears invading our neighborhoods, it might help to remember that we invaded their neighborhoods first.
meaning	

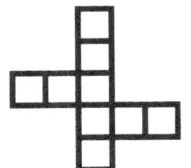

Word Clues #2
Making Inferences

ANSWERS

Word	Sentences
canid	Bears have developed a fear of (canids.) A barking, snarling <u>dog</u> looks just as dangerous to a mother bear as a <u>wolf or coyote</u>.
meaning	Canids are animals in the dog family.
co-exist	Most people who live in bear country feel that if humans were more careful, they could <u>peacefully</u> (co-exist) with bears. Although most residents have learned <u>to live in harmony</u> with bears and even consider them their neighbors, more and more people are moving into bear country from the city.
meaning	Co-exist means to live in harmony and peace with others.
retract	You can (retract) the lead and <u>pull it back</u> in by pushing a button, but it isn't easy in an emergency to do this quickly.
meaning	Retract means to pull something back.
habitat	Bear (habitats) are shrinking because humans are <u>moving into them</u>. When we get upset about bears invading <u>our neighborhoods</u>, it might help to remember that we invaded <u>their neighborhoods</u> first.
meaning	Habitats are the places where humans or animals live.

Word Clues #3
Opposite Meanings
based on *Hank the Tank*
by Carolee Dean

DIRECTIONS: Circle the target word in the sentence. Underline the hints that help you understand the meaning. Write down what you think the meaning is based on the hints.

BEWARE: Sometimes the context tells us the **opposite** of what the word means. Look for negative words like **no, don't, instead, lose,** or **unfortunately** as a clue that the information may hinting at the opposite meaning.

Word	Sentences
hibernate	When bears can easily find donuts in dumpsters, candy bars in cars, and casseroles left in cabins, there is no need to hibernate. As a result, some bears stay awake all winter.
meaning:	.
instinct	When a bear loses its instincts, it has unnatural impulses to do things like eat garbage.
ransack	Unfortunately, we had to spend the day cleaning up the mess after the bear ransacked our house.
nibs	I would rather have a big chunk of chocolate instead of nibs.

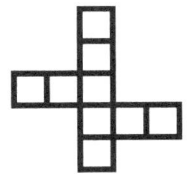

Word Clues #3
Opposite Meanings
based on *Hank the Tank*
by Carolee Dean

ANSWERS

Word	Sentences
hibernate	When bears can easily find donuts in dumpsters, candy bars in cars, and casseroles left in cabins, there is <u>no need to</u> (hibernate.) As a result, some <u>bears stay awake all winter.</u>
meaning:	*Hibernate means to sleep all winter.*
instinct	When a bear <u>loses its</u> (instincts,) it has <u>unnatural impulses</u> to do things like eat garbage.
Meaning:	*Instincts are natural impulses.*
ransack	<u>Unfortunately,</u> we had to spend the day <u>picking up the mess</u> after the bear (ransacked) our house.
meaning:	*Ransack means to make a mess.*
nibs	I would rather have a big chunk of chocolate instead of (nibs.)
meaning:	*Nibs are little bits of chocolate.*

Word Clues #4
Snack Attack Word Mash-Up
based on *Hank the Tank*
by Carolee Dean

Sometimes you can find clues to a word's meaning right inside of the word. This is especially true for new food combinations. Look at the words below. Two foods have been combined to make a new food and a new word.

Directions: Make a list of snack foods on a separate piece of paper. Take two foods from your list and make a new food combination. Describe your new food and give it a name. Create a total of three new snack foods.

Food #1	Food #2	Name it	Describe it
tater tots	nachos	totchos	Nachos made with tater tots instead of tortilla chips.
grub (food)	rubbish (trash)	grubbish	Junk food

Scavenger Hunts

Explain the concept of **scavenger** to students.

Some scavengers are animals, and some are humans.

A bear is an animal that is a scavenger. Animal scavengers eat dead things they **find** lying around like carrion (dead animals) and rotten food.

A human scavenger collects things they **find** that others have thrown away or left behind.

A scavenger hunt is a game where people must **find** items on a list.

For the next set of activities, students will be hunting for words and phrases found in the book, *Hank the Tank*. After **finding** all of the words, the student uses the letter clues to reveal the secret message at the bottom of the page.

Hint: If a letter is repeated, the number that goes with it will appear more than once.

Scavenger Hunt #1 - from Part 1
Scavenger Hunt #2 – from Part 2
Scavenger Hunt #3 – from Part 3
Scavenger Hunt #4 – from Part 4
Scavenger Hunt #5 – from Parts 1-4.

Scavenger Hunt #1

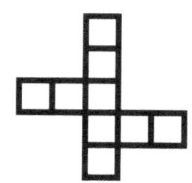

Directions: Reread Part 1 of the rhyming story about *Hank the Tank.* Find the lines below from the poem. Then write down the words that complete the phrase or sentence. When you have found all the words, use the letter clues to reveal the secret message at the bottom of the page. The first line has been completed for you. Notice how some of the numbers repeat.

Clacking racks and
s m a c k i n g   l i p s
1 2 3 4 5 6 7 8   9 6 10 1

French dip sandwich, bag of
  c   i p s
4 11 6 10 1

Pollock and a
s   c   i s
1 11 12 - 4 13 14 15   16 6 1 11

Hush! Be still until he
    i   s
17 18 6 19 1

Now use the number clues above to reveal the secret message below.

p i   k   p   s
10 6 4 5   18 10   19 13 14 1 11

Scavenger Hunt #1

ANSWERS

Clacking racks and

s m a c k i n g   l i p s
1 2 3 4 5 6 7 8   9 6 10 1

French dip sandwich, bag of

c h i p s
4 11 6 10 1

Pollock and a

s h e - c r a b   d i s h
1 11 12 4 13 14 15   16 6 1 11

Hush! Be still until he

q u i t s
17 18 6 19 1

Now use the number clues above to reveal the secret message below.

p i c k u p t r a s h
10 6 4 5 18 10 19 13 14 1 11

Scavenger Hunt #2

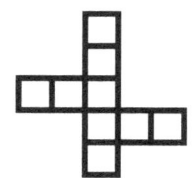

Directions: Reread Part 2 of the rhyming story about *Hank the Tank.* Find the lines below from the poem. Then write down the words that complete the phrase or sentence. When you have found all the words, use the letter clues to reveal the secret message at the bottom of the page. The first line has been completed for you.

1. I suspect the $\underset{1}{\text{T}}\ \underset{2}{\text{a}}\ \underset{3}{\text{n}}\ \underset{4}{\text{k}}$ is back.

2. He's ___ ___ ___ ___ ___ ___ ___ ___ on a bunch of ___ ___ ___ ___
        5 6 3 7 8 9 3 10   11 9 12 13

   with ___ ___ ___ ___ ___ ___ ___ and a sack of nibs.
        4 14 1 7 8 15 16

3. Hank's ___ ___ ___ quick, but he has strength. Heft and ___ ___ ___ ___.
        3 17 1   12 6 18 4

   Width and length.

Now use the number clues above to reveal the secret message below.

___ ___ ___ ___   ___ ___ ___   ___ ___ ___ ___ ___ ___
18 17 7 4   1 8 14   1 11 6 7 4 13

Scavenger Hunt #2

ANSWERS

1. I suspect the **T** **a** **n** **k** is back.
               1 2 3 4

2. He's **m** **u** **n** **c** **h** **i** **n** **g** on a bunch of **r** **i** **b** **s**
        5 6 3 7 8 9 3 10   11 9 12 13

with **k** **e** **t** **c** **h** **u** **p** and a sack of nibs.
       4 14 1 7 8 15 16

3. Hank's **n** **o** **t** quick, but he has strength. Heft and **b** **u** **l** **k**.
      3 17 1   12 6 18 4

Width and length.

Now use the number clues above to reveal the secret message below.

l **o** **c** **k**   **t** **h** **e**   **t** **r** **u** **c** **k** **s**
18 17 7 4   1 8 14   1 11 6 7 4 13

Scavenger Hunt #3

Directions: Reread Part 3 of the rhyming story about *Hank the Tank.* Find the words on the right below. Then write down the word that comes just BEFORE that word in the story. When you have found all the words, use the letter clues to reveal the secret message at the bottom of the page. The first line has been completed for you.

1. $\underset{1}{k}\ \underset{2}{i}\ \underset{3}{t}\ \underset{4}{c}\ \underset{5}{h}\ \underset{6}{e}\ \underset{7}{n}$ sink

2. $\underset{8}{\_\_}\ \underset{9}{\_\_}\ \underset{10}{\_\_}\ \underset{11}{\_\_}\ \underset{8}{\_\_}$ hams

3. $\underset{12}{\_\_}\ \underset{6}{\_\_}\ \underset{13}{\_\_}$ gumdrops

4. $\underset{14}{\_\_}\ \underset{3}{\_\_}\ \underset{15}{\_\_}\ \underset{4}{\_\_}\ \underset{1}{\_\_}$ pot (p. 30)

5. $\underset{11}{\_\_}\ \underset{16}{\_\_}\ \underset{7}{\_\_}\ \underset{17}{\_\_}\ \underset{15}{\_\_}$ whips (p. 27)

6. $\underset{18}{\_\_}\ \underset{9}{\_\_}\ \underset{16}{\_\_}\ \underset{4}{\_\_}\ \underset{1}{\_\_}$ chopsticks

Now use the number clues above to reveal the secret message below.

$\underset{14}{\_\_}\ \underset{4}{\_\_}\ \underset{12}{\_\_}\ \underset{10}{\_\_}\ \underset{18}{\_\_}\ \ \ \ \underset{3}{\_\_}\ \underset{5}{\_\_}\ \underset{6}{\_\_}\ \ \ \ \underset{17}{\_\_}\ \underset{12}{\_\_}\ \underset{2}{\_\_}\ \underset{9}{\_\_}\ \underset{9}{\_\_}$

Scavenger Hunt #3

ANSWERS

1. **k i t c h e n**
    ___ ___ ___ ___ ___ ___ ___   sink
    1   2   3   4   5   6   7

2. **p l u m p**
    ___ ___ ___ ___ ___   hams
    8   9   10 11 8

3. **r e d**
    ___ ___ ___   gumdrops
    12 6   13

4. **s t o c k**
    ___ ___ ___ ___ ___   pot
    14 3   15 4   1

5. **m a n g o**
    ___ ___ ___ ___ ___   whips
    11 16 7   17 15

6. **b l a c k**
    ___ ___ ___ ___ ___   chopsticks
    18 9   16 4   1

Now use the number clues above to reveal the secret message below.

s c r u b   **t h e**   **g r i l l**
___ ___ ___ ___ ___   ___ ___ ___   ___ ___ ___ ___ ___
14 4   12 10 18   3   5   6   17 12 2   9   9

Scavenger Hunt #4

Directions: Reread Part 4 of the rhyming story about *Hank the Tank.* Find the words and phrases below. Then write down the missing words. Most come just BEFORE the word that you see. When you have found all the words, use the letter clues to reveal the secret message at the bottom of the page. The first line has been completed for you.

1. g r u b b i s h mess
    1 2 3 4 4 5 6 7

2. Go hunt for ___ ___ ___ ___
                8 5 6 7

3. ___ ___ ___ dish
   9 10 1

4. b
  ___ ___ ___ ___ ___ string (p. 39)
  4 11 12 13 14

5. ___ ___ ___ ___ ___ ___ trap
  15 3 16 16 17 11

Now use the number clues above to reveal the secret message below.

___ ___ ___ ___ ___   ___ ___ ___ ___   ___ ___ ___ ___ ___
9 10   16 10 15   8 17 17 9   4 17 12 2 6

Scavenger Hunt #4

ANSWERS

1. **g r u b b i s h**
   1 2 3 4 4 5 6 7   mess

2. Go hunt for   **f i s h**
   8 5 6 7

3. **d o g**
   9 10 1   dish

4. **b l a c k**
   4 11 12 13 14   string

5. **t u n n e l**
   15 3 16 16 17 11   trap

Now use the number clues above to reveal the secret message below.

D o   **n o t**   **f e e d**   **b e a r s**
9 10   16 10 15   8 17 17 9   4 17 12 2 6

Scavenger Hunt #5

Directions: Reread the entire rhyming story about *Hank the Tank.* Find the word (or words) below. Write down the word that comes AFTER it in the story. Then use the letter clues to reveal the secret message at the bottom of the page.

clacking ___ ___ ___ ___ ___ (p. 13)
　　　　　 1　 2　 3　 4　 5

Atlantic ___ ___ ___ ___
　　　　　 6　 7　 5　 8

picnic ___ ___ ___ ___ ___ ___ (p. 23)
　　　　 9　 2　 5　 4　 10　 11

stock ___ ___ ___
　　　　 12　 13　 11

bonging ___ ___ ___ ___ ___ (p. 37)
　　　　　 14　 10　 15　 15　 5

smack it ___ ___ ___ ___ ___
　　　　　 16　 8　 2　 18　 4

Watch him ___ ___ ___ ___
　　　　　　 17　 2　 5　 8

Now use the number clues above to figure out the secret message below.

___ ___ ___ ___ ___ ___ ___ ___ ___ ___ ___ ___ ___
 4　 10　 10　 12　 14　 10　 2　 1　 5　 16　 7　 15　 17

Scavenger Hunt #5

ANSWERS

	r	a	c	k	s	
clacking	1	2	3	4	5	

	f	i	s	h		
Atlantic	6	7	5	8		

	b	a	s	k	e	t
picnic	9	2	5	4	10	11

	p	o	t			
stock	12	13	11			

	b	e	l	l	s	
bonging	14	10	15	15	5	

	w	h	a	c	k	
smack it	16	8	2	17	4	

	d	a	s	h		
Watch him	18	2	5	8		

Now use the number clues above to figure out the secret message below.

k	e	e	p	b	e	a	r	s	w	i	l	d
4	10	10	12	14	10	2	1	5	16	7	15	18

Multiple Meaning Match Up
based on *Hank the Tank*
by Carolee Dean

Directions: 1. Make two copies of the words below.
2 Cut out the words and glue them onto construction paper.
3. Play the Memory Matching game.   4. Make sure you choose words with
the same meanings.

bear hold up, carry, support, endure	**bear** a big furry animal	**sap** a silly or foolish person
sap a sticky fluid from a tree	**scat** wild animal poop	**scat** go away, leave
check inspect or look at something	**check** used in place of cash	**drumstick** a food, the leg of a chicken
drumstick used for beating a drum	**watch** observe or look at	**watch** used to tell time
chest part of the upper body	**chest** a box with a lid used to store things	

WOW Vocabulary Terms #1
From the Story
based on *Hank the Tank*
by Carolee Dean

These cards may be used in a variety of ways.
Choose an option from the VOCABULARY CARD OPTIONS page.

assist	lot	shallot
co-exist	mango	slops
concoct	millet	squid
DNA	nibs	totchos
fennel	pollock	whelk
grubbish	rubbish	whisk
heft	sap	
hutch	scat	

WOW Vocabulary Terms #2
From the BACKGROUND INFORMATION
based on *Hank the Tank*
by Carolee Dean

These cards may be used in a variety of ways. Choose an option from the VOCABULARY CARD OPTIONS page.

		moniker
adapt	euthanize	motion detector
adolescent	eyewitness	nuisance
attractant	fluctuate	predator
binge	habitat	prey
canid	haze	ransack
canine	hibernate	rummage
chest blaze	hyperphagia	scavenger
culvert trap	instinct	tranquilize

WOW Vocabulary Terms
Blank Pages
Invent Your Own

These cards may be used in a variety of ways.
Choose an option from the **VOCABULARY CARD OPTIONS** page.

WOW Vocabulary #3
Idioms

based on *Hank the Tank*
by Carolee Dean

1. Study the idioms below.
2. Use them to make a vocabulary foldable.

Word	Meaning
*Bear market	When stock market prices are falling and investors are trying to sell.
Hungry as a bear	Very hungry.
Busy as a hibernating bear	Not busy.
A real bear	A situation or person that is difficult.
Bear-hug	A tight embrace.
Bear claw	A large pastry.
Be a Teddy Bear	A person who is kind and sweet on the inside. They may or may not appear tough on the outside.
Poke the bear	To offend or make some angry on purpose.

*from www.etymonline.com – relates to an old proverb about the dangers of selling the bearskin before one has caught the bear.

Vocabulary Foldable
based on *Hank the Tank*
by Carolee Dean

Directions:

1. Write (or cut and paste) 8 words from the WOW Vocabulary List on a blank vocabulary foldable. The first one has been done for you.

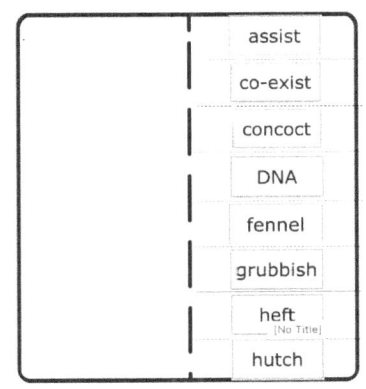

2. Then cut on the dotted lines between the words.

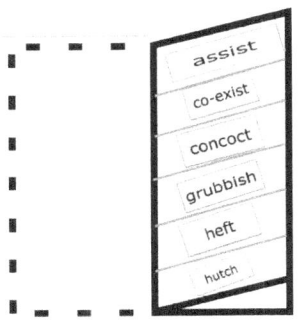

3. Fold the paper in half lengthwise.

4. Open the foldable and write the definitions for the words on the inside on the right. Draw pictures to go with the word on the left. You can find the definitions in the book, *Hank the Tank*.

5. Close the foldable. Test yourself by reading a word out loud. Say the definition. Then open the foldable and see if you were right.

6. When you are done studying the words and definitions cut them apart, glue them onto construction paper, and play a memory matching game.

Definitions

to help

live in peace

to make

.

Vocabulary Foldable
based on *Hank the Tank*
by Carolee Dean

assist

co-exist

concoct

DNA

fennel

grubbish

heft

hutch

Vocabulary Foldable
Blank
based on *Hank the Tank*
by Carolee Dean

SENTENCE AWARENESS

INTRODUCTION – ING Verbs

Use the information on the following pages to explain the concepts to your students.

-ING is a suffix that shows verb tense: *packing, jumping, camping*. It is often found with a "to be" helping verb: **am, is, are, was, were, been.**

I **am** snacking. He **is** snacking They **are** snacking. She **was** snacking. They **were** snacking. I have **been** snacking.

Sometimes an –ing verb can morph or change. When it does this, it might turn into an adjective. Test out the sentences below to see if you can replace the –ing word with an adjective like *red, big, good*, or *soft*. If you can, then the –ing word is acting like an adjective.

He is <u>walking</u> up the stairs. He took his <u>walking</u> stick on a hike.
She went <u>shopping</u> on Sunday. She set the can in the <u>shopping</u> bag.

(He took his <u>big</u> stick on a hike. She set the can in the <u>red</u> bag.)

Sometimes an –ing verb can even turn into a noun. Is it an action, or is it a thing? If it is a thing, it is a noun.

She was <u>frosting</u> the cake. She ate the <u>frosting</u>.

Sentence Mania Activity: Students will explore helping verbs and learn how verbs can be used as adjectives. Although this is a sentence activity, you may want to introduce it when the student is learning about –ing endings in the morphology section. This activity is also available in a Boom Card Format for an additional fee at https://wow.boomlearning.com. Go to **Store>Word Travel Press.** The cards from the Boom Deck are available here if you would like to further explore this activity as a board game. When playing the game, students state if the –ing word is acting like a VERB or an ADJECTIVE. They then state the **helping verb** if the –ing word is a verb or the **noun** being modified if the –ing word is an adjective.

Sentence Mania
Part 1
based on *Hank the Tank*
by Carolee Dean

Directions: Circle VERB if the –ing word is acting like a VERB. Draw an arrow under the helping verb (am, is, are, was, were).
Circle ADJECTIVE if the –ing word it is acting like an ADJECTIVE. Put a box around the noun it modifies.

EXAMPLES:

1. Beth plans to go to a <u>cooking</u> class on Thursday.   Verb   ⟨Adjective⟩

2. Seth is <u>cooking</u> pizza for dinner.   ⟨Verb⟩   Adjective

HINT: What is Beth doing in sentence number 1? She is NOT cooking. She is planning on attending a class about cooking.

Word	Part of Speech	
1. Hank is <u>shocking</u> the kids.	Verb	Adjective
2. He left bits of <u>shocking</u> things.	Verb	Adjective
3. The trash is <u>stinking</u> up the room.	Verb	Adjective
4. The <u>stinking</u> bandit ate a snack.	Verb	Adjective
5. He is <u>going</u> into the hills.	Verb	Adjective
6. I set the stick on the <u>ticking</u> clock.	Verb	Adjective
7. Hank is <u>splashing</u> in the kitchen sink.	Verb	Adjective
8. She left a <u>drinking</u> glass on the bench.	Verb	Adjective
9. He is <u>drinking</u> punch.	Verb	Adjective
10. My pants are <u>shrinking.</u>	Verb	Adjective

Sentence Mania
Part 1
based on *Hank the Tank*
by Carolee Dean

ANSWERS

Word	Part of Speech
1. Hank is <u>shocking</u> the kids.	**(Verb)** Adjective
2. He left bits of <u>shocking</u> things.	Verb **(Adjective)**
3. The trash is <u>stinking</u> up the room.	**(Verb)** Adjective
4. The <u>stinking</u> bandit ate a snack.	Verb **(Adjective)**
5. He is <u>going</u> into the hills.	**(Verb)** Adjective
6. I set the stick on the <u>ticking</u> clock.	Verb **(Adjective)**
7. Hank is <u>splashing</u> in the kitchen sink.	**(Verb)** Adjective
8. She left a <u>drinking</u> glass on the bench.	Verb **(Adjective)**
9. He is <u>drinking</u> punch.	**(Verb)** Adjective
10. My pants are <u>shrinking</u>.	**(Verb)** Adjective

Sentence Mania
Part 2
based on *Hank the Tank*
by Carolee Dean

Directions: Circle VERB if the –ing word is acting like a VERB. Draw an arrow under the helping verb (am, is, are, was, were).
Circle ADJECTIVE if the –ing word it is acting like an ADJECTIVE. Put a box around the noun it modifies.

Word	Part of Speech	
11. She hid the <u>frosting</u> can.	Verb	Adjective
12. We are <u>packing</u> the tent.	Verb	Adjective
13. Gunk was <u>hanging</u> from his chin.	Verb	Adjective
14. Did he smash the <u>hanging</u> plants?	Verb	Adjective
15. He took his <u>fishing</u> pole to the pond.	Verb	Adjective
16. He set the ham on the <u>chopping</u> block.	Verb	Adjective
17. He is <u>chopping</u> the ham.	Verb	Adjective
18. They put a <u>tracking</u> tag on the bear.	Verb	Adjective
19. They are <u>tracking</u> the bear.	Verb	Adjective
20. Hank the Tank is <u>snatching</u> lunch.	Verb	Adjective

Sentence Mania
Part 2
based on *Hank the Tank*
by Carolee Dean

ANSWERS

Word	Part of Speech
11. She hid the <u>frosting</u> can.	Verb · **(Adjective)**
12. We are <u>packing</u> the tent.	**(Verb)** · Adjective
13. Gunk was <u>hanging</u> from his chin.	**(Verb)** · Adjective
14. Did he smash the <u>hanging</u> plants?	Verb · **(Adjective)**
15. He took his <u>fishing</u> pole to the pond.	Verb · **(Adjective)**
16. He set the ham on the <u>chopping</u> block.	Verb · **(Adjective)**
17. He is <u>chopping</u> the ham.	**(Verb)** · Adjective
18. They put a <u>tracking</u> tag on the bear.	Verb · **(Adjective)**
19. They are <u>tracking</u> the bear.	**(Verb)** · Adjective
20. Hank the Tank is <u>snatching</u> lunch.	**(Verb)** · Adjective

Sentence Mania - GAME CARDS

Directions: Cut out the cards below and use them with the Hank Game Board. When playing the game, students state if the –ing word is acting like a VERB or an ADJECTIVE. They then state the **helping verb (**if the –ing word is a verb) or the **noun** being modified (if it is an adjective). This activity is also available in a Boom Card Format.

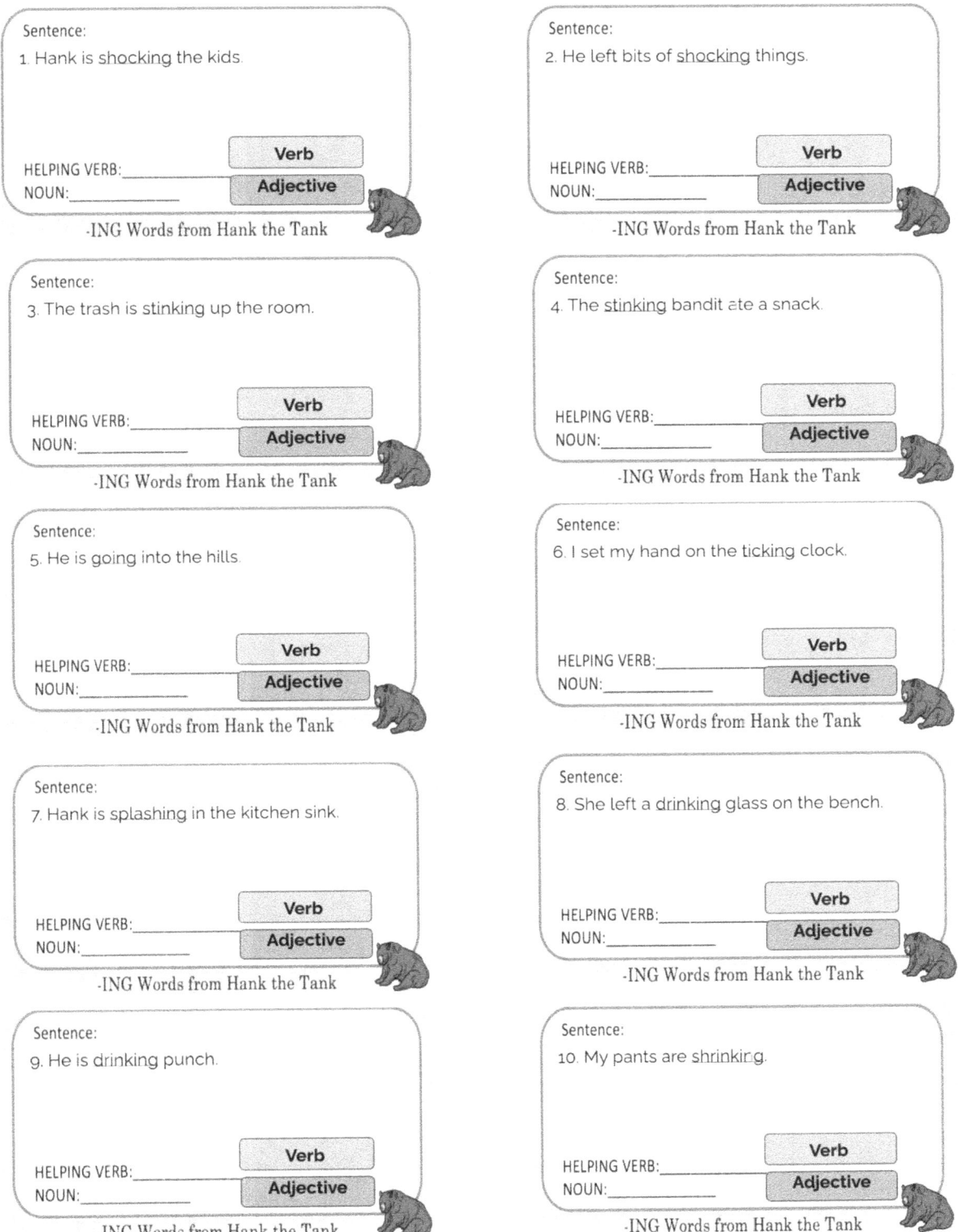

Sentence:

1. Hank is shocking the kids.

HELPING VERB:_____ **Verb**
NOUN:_____ **Adjective**

-ING Words from Hank the Tank

Sentence:

2. He left bits of shocking things.

HELPING VERB:_____ **Verb**
NOUN:_____ **Adjective**

-ING Words from Hank the Tank

Sentence:

3. The trash is stinking up the room.

HELPING VERB:_____ **Verb**
NOUN:_____ **Adjective**

-ING Words from Hank the Tank

Sentence:

4. The stinking bandit ate a snack.

HELPING VERB:_____ **Verb**
NOUN:_____ **Adjective**

-ING Words from Hank the Tank

Sentence:

5. He is going into the hills.

HELPING VERB:_____ **Verb**
NOUN:_____ **Adjective**

-ING Words from Hank the Tank

Sentence:

6. I set my hand on the ticking clock.

HELPING VERB:_____ **Verb**
NOUN:_____ **Adjective**

-ING Words from Hank the Tank

Sentence:

7. Hank is splashing in the kitchen sink.

HELPING VERB:_____ **Verb**
NOUN:_____ **Adjective**

-ING Words from Hank the Tank

Sentence:

8. She left a drinking glass on the bench.

HELPING VERB:_____ **Verb**
NOUN:_____ **Adjective**

-ING Words from Hank the Tank

Sentence:

9. He is drinking punch.

HELPING VERB:_____ **Verb**
NOUN:_____ **Adjective**

-ING Words from Hank the Tank

Sentence:

10. My pants are shrinking.

HELPING VERB:_____ **Verb**
NOUN:_____ **Adjective**

-ING Words from Hank the Tank

Sentence Mania - GAME CARDS

Directions: Cut out the cards below and use them with the game board. When playing the game, students state if the –ing word is acting like a VERB or an ADJECTIVE. They then state the **helping verb (**if the –ing word is a verb) or the **noun** being modified (if it is an adjective).

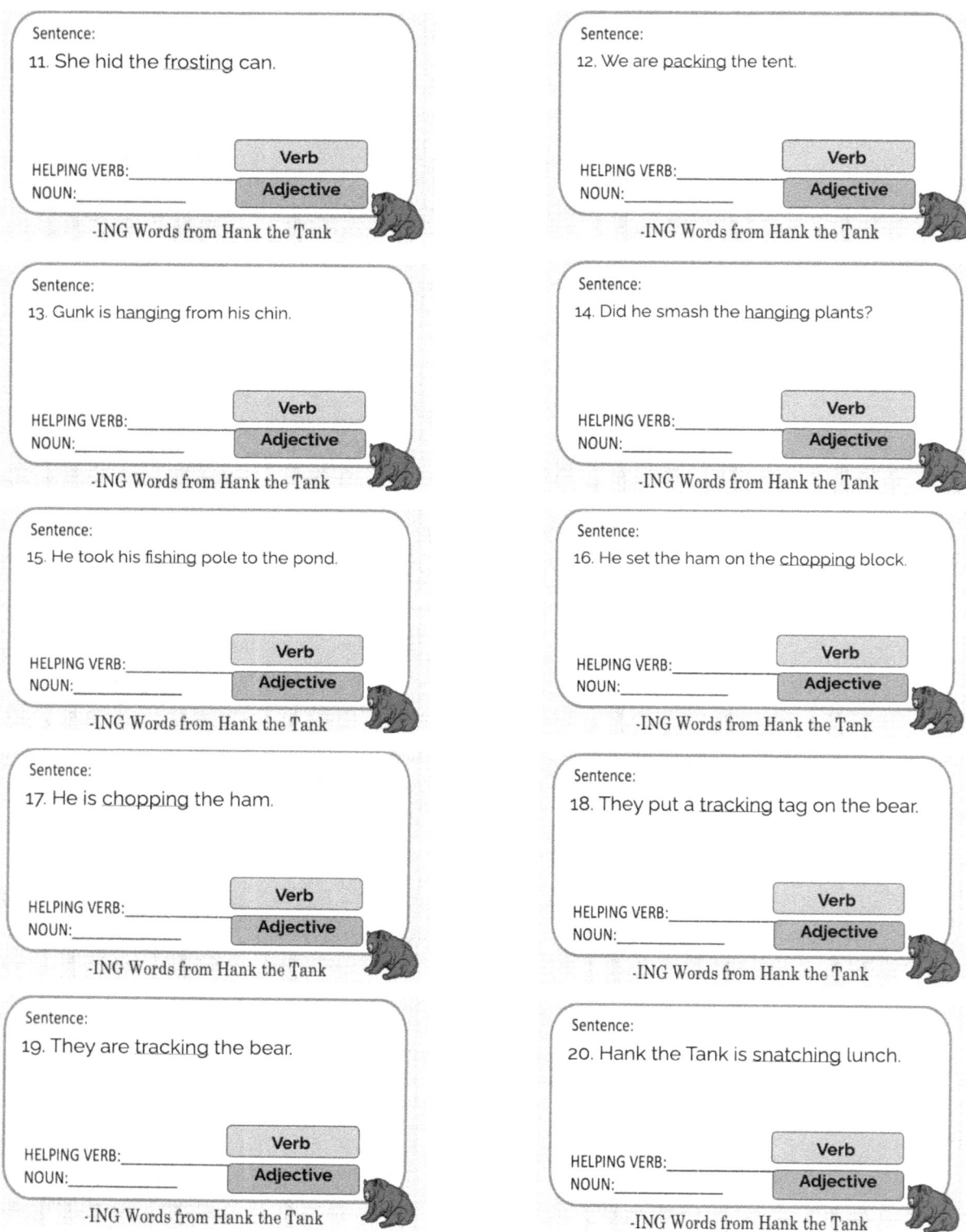

Sentence:

11. She hid the <u>frosting</u> can.

HELPING VERB:_____
NOUN:_____

Verb

Adjective

-ING Words from Hank the Tank

Sentence:

12. We are <u>packing</u> the tent.

HELPING VERB:_____
NOUN:_____

Verb

Adjective

-ING Words from Hank the Tank

Sentence:

13. Gunk is <u>hanging</u> from his chin.

HELPING VERB:_____
NOUN:_____

Verb

Adjective

-ING Words from Hank the Tank

Sentence:

14. Did he smash the <u>hanging</u> plants?

HELPING VERB:_____
NOUN:_____

Verb

Adjective

-ING Words from Hank the Tank

Sentence:

15. He took his <u>fishing</u> pole to the pond.

HELPING VERB:_____
NOUN:_____

Verb

Adjective

-ING Words from Hank the Tank

Sentence:

16. He set the ham on the <u>chopping</u> block.

HELPING VERB:_____
NOUN:_____

Verb

Adjective

-ING Words from Hank the Tank

Sentence:

17. He is <u>chopping</u> the ham.

HELPING VERB:_____
NOUN:_____

Verb

Adjective

-ING Words from Hank the Tank

Sentence:

18. They put a <u>tracking</u> tag on the bear.

HELPING VERB:_____
NOUN:_____

Verb

Adjective

-ING Words from Hank the Tank

Sentence:

19. They are <u>tracking</u> the bear.

HELPING VERB:_____
NOUN:_____

Verb

Adjective

-ING Words from Hank the Tank

Sentence:

20. Hank the Tank is <u>snatching</u> lunch.

HELPING VERB:_____
NOUN:_____

Verb

Adjective

-ING Words from Hank the Tank

SENTENCE CONSTRUCTION

INTRODUCTION

Many students, even those without reading challenges, have difficulty determining if a sentence is complete or incomplete. Part of the reason is that most kids are taught that a sentence must have a noun and a verb. Unfortunately, confusion arises with words that can be both nouns and verbs as we saw on the previous pages.

Before starting the sentence construction activities, talk with students about the meaning of the terms *Subject* and *Predicate*. Looking at sentences this way is more consistent than using terms like *Nouns* and *Verbs*. Also, discuss with students how poetry is not always written in complete sentences even when there is a period at the end of a line. For more information about sentence writing, visit the website at www.wordtravelpress.com and see the page for COR Instruction.

Sentence Construction #1: Sentence Combining: Students use the conjunctions that are provided to create longer sentences. Demonstrate for them how the period turns into a comma if the information that comes after it could stand alone as a sentence. Technically, if the second part is short, a comma is not always needed, but for this activity, we will use it. Sentence combining is an activity that improves both reading and writing skills. Since decodable books often contain short, choppy sentences, it is important to provide experiences with longer sentences. A related activity focusing on comma usage is available in a Boom Card Format for an additional fee at https://wow.boomlearning.com and **Store>Word Travel Press.**

Sentence Construction #2: Who is Doing What? - Students ask Wh- questions about an illustration from the book to create one long sentence.

Sentence Construction #3: Identifying Complete Sentences - Students determine if sentences are complete or incomplete and then decide if a subject or predicate is missing. On a separate piece of paper, instruct them to choose a sentence fragment and add what is missing (subject or predicate) to turn the fragment into a complete sentence.

References:
Hochman, J.C. & MacDermott-Duffy, B. (2018). Composition: Evidence-based instruction. In J.R. Birsh & S. Carreker (Eds.) *Multisensory teaching of basic language skills* (4th ed., pp. 205-253). Baltimore, MD: Paul H. Brookes Publishing Co.

Nelson, N.W. (2013). Syntax development in the school-age years: implications for assessment and intervention. *Perspectives on Language and Literacy*. 39 (3), 9-15.

Van Cleave, W. (2014). *Writing matters: Developing sentence skills in students of all ages (Second Edition)*. Greenville, SC: W.V.C.ED

Sentence Construction #1
Sentence Combining
based on *Hank the Tank*
by Carolee Dean

Directions:
Use the conjunction in **bold** to combine the 2 short sentences.

Example:
(and) The dog can run. The dog can bark.
The dog can run, and it can bark.   OR
The dog can run and bark.

(for) The bear broke into the car. The bear was hungry.

(and) The bear ate fish. The bear ate chips.

(nor) The bear did not bite. The bear did not attack.

(but) The kids scared the bear away. The bear came back.

(or) You can scrub the deck. You can scrub the grill.

(yet) A pet door may be small. A bear might still climb through it.

(so) DNA proved there were three bears. Hank's life was saved.

Sentence Construction #1
Sentence Combining
based on *Hank the Tank*
by Carolee Dean

POSSIBLE ANSWERS
Responses may vary

(for) The bear broke into the car. The bear was hungry.

The bear broke into the car, for it was hungry.

(and) The bear ate fish. The bear ate chips.
The bear ate fish, and it ate chips.
The bear ate fish and chips.

(nor) The bear did not bite. The bear did not attack.
The bear did not bite, nor did it attack.
The bear did not bite nor attack.

(but) The kids scared the bear away. The bear came back.
The kids scared the bear away, but it came back

(or) You can scrub the deck. You can clean scrub.
You can scrub the deck, or you can scrub the grill.
You can scrub the deck or the grill.

(yet) A pet door may be small. A bear might still climb through it.
A pet door may be small, yet a bear might still climb through it.

(so) DNA proved there were three bears. Hank's life was saved.
DNA proved there were three bears, so Hank's life was saved.

Note: If "therefore" can be used in place of "so" then use a comma.
   If "so that" can be used in place of "so" then do NOT use a comma.

Example: They collected DNA so they could prove who was responsible.
   (No comma)

Sentence Construction #2
Who is Doing What?
based on *Hank the Tank*
by Carolee Dean

Directions:
1. Look at the illustration in Part 4 of the story where two people are standing next to the culvert trap.
2. Describe what is going on in the illustration by answering the questions.
3. Use your answers to construct one long sentence on the lines below.

Question   **Response**

1. Who is in the illustration?

2. What are they doing?

3. How are they it doing it?
(ex. quickly, quietly, with caution).

4. When is it happening?
(one morning, last summer)

5. Where is it happening?

6. Why is it happening?

_____

_____

_____
\

_____

Sentence Construction #3
Identifying Complete Sentences
based on *Hank the Tank*
by Carolee Dean

A complete sentence requires two things: a SUBJECT (Who or What is doing) + a PREDICATE (What they are doing)

Directions:
1. Read each line below. Is it a complete sentence? Circle YES or NO.
2. If NO - circle SUBJECT or PREDICATE (Verb) to show what is missing.
3. On a separate piece of paper, pick an incomplete sentence below. Add information to make it complete.

Line of Verse	Complete Sentence		What's Missing?	
1. Lids are banging in the kitchen.	yes	no	subject	predicate
2. The clunking bandit.	yes	no	subject	predicate
3. He sniffs a lid.	yes	no	subject	predicate
4. Licks the trash.	yes	no	subject	predicate
5. That gut of his.	yes	no	subject	predicate
6. Men in hats set traps.	yes	no	subject	predicate
7. Checking for DNA.	yes	no	subject	predicate
8. Beth grabs the plums.	yes	no	subject	predicate
9. Is snacking.	yes	no	subject	predicate
10. A vandal.	yes	no	subject	predicate

Sentence Construction #3
Identifying Complete Sentences
based on *Hank the Tank*
by Carolee Dean

ANSWERS

Line of Verse	Complete Sentence		What's Missing?	
1. Lids are banging in the kitchen.	(yes)	no	subject	predicate
2. The clunking bandit.	yes	(no)	subject	(predicate)
3. He sniffs a lid.	(yes)	no	subject	predicate
4. Licks the trash.	yes	(no	subject)	predicate
5. That gut of his.	yes	(no)	subject	(predicate)
6. Men in hats set traps.	(yes)	no	subject	predicate
7. Checking for DNA.	yes	(no	subject)	predicate
8. Beth grabs the plums.	(yes)	no	subject	predicate
9. Is snacking.	yes	(no	subject)	predicate
10. A vandal.	yes	(no)	subject	(predicate)

STORY FRAMES

Story Frames

INTRODUCTION

The Story Analysis described in the following pages is based on my book, *Story Frames for Teaching Literacy: Enhancing Student Learning Through the Power of Storytelling* (Paul H. Brookes Publishing Co., 2021). That book is not needed to complete this story analysis but if you would like to take a deeper dive into narrative intervention with access to 35 adaptable lesson plans along with downloadable resources, you can find my book at Brookes Publishing. The lesson plans include a more detailed approach to summary writing as well as a discussion of how writing expectations change across the grade levels.

Storytelling is an important part of oral discourse for young children. This skill supports the ability to read and understand narratives during the school years. Fundamental to comprehension is the ability to put information into a schema. Understanding text structure helps students to know if they should be organizing the information into the framework of a story, a poem, a non-fiction information article, and so forth. In addition, students practice Theory of Mind when they are asked to determine an author's purpose or take the point of view of a character. Many speech-language pathologists use narratives as the basis of their language interventions because every other component of language may be addressed through the content and context of a story. That concept has been demonstrated by the range of activities in this Activity Book used to explore one story.

After reading the story, the student uses the blank version of the BASIC STORYBOARD and draws stick figures, writes keywords, or both in each square to show what is happening in each frame of the story. Model as needed. This step may be completed as a class, small group, with a partner, or individually. The completed storyboard may then be used to retell the story verbally or to write a summary. Help students decide which vocabulary terms to write at the bottom. If a student is listening to the story read aloud, they may use the pictography strategy described by Ukrainetz (1998) to draw the action of the story in stick figures on a blank piece of paper. These figures may be cut or redrawn into the sections of the Storyboard.

References:
Dean, C. (2021). Story frames for teaching literacy: Enhancing student learning through the power of storytelling. Baltimore, MD: Paul H. Brookes Publishing Co.

Stein, N., & Glenn, C. (1979). An analysis of story comprehension in elementary school children. In R. Freedle (Ed.), New directions in discourse processing (Vol. 2, pp. 53-120). Norwood, NJ: Ablex.

Ukrainetz, T. (1998). Stickwriting stories: A quick and easy narrative representation strategy. *Language, Speech, and Hearing in Schools*, 29, 197-206.

Plot Analysis

HANK THE TANK

ORDINARY WORLD – Seth and his sister, Beth, are two teens who live in the Tahoe Keys area in California.

CALL & RESPONSE – One day a bear breaks into their house. It keeps coming back. The first time they just wait for it to leave. The second time they make loud noises and scare it away.

PROBLEM & PRIZE – The problem is that the bear is attracted to the food and trash in their house. The "prize" is to figure out how to keep the bear from breaking in and ransacking their property.

PLAN – The kids plan to get rid of attractants.

ATTEMPT – The kids and their parents clean up the yard. They take the dog food inside, clean the grill, pick up rotting fruit, sweep, etc.

ATTEMPT – The kids record annoying sounds that will play if the bear comes near their house and steps on a trip wire. The recording works and scares the bear away. He heads for a tunnel trap but does not go inside.

CLIMAX – Very soon the bear is back, but it is not the same bear. The kids see more bears nearby. They realize there were actually three bears involved in the break-ins.

REWARD – The children learn what to do so that they can peacefully co-exist with the bears in their neighborhood.

Story Frames (Basic Version) – HANK THE TANK by Carolee Dean

Ordinary World	Call & Response	Problem & Prize	Plan

Attempt		Climax	Reward

Attempt

Vocabulary	People & Places	Conjunctions		Transitions	
		because	even if	first	eventually
		although	when	next	consequently
		before	whenever	last	surprisingly
		after	where	in addition	finally
		unless	while	as a result	

©2023 Word Travel Press LLC - based on activities from *Story Frames for Teaching Literacy* (Brookes Publishing, 2021)

COMPREHENSION

INTRODUCTION

PAGES – The PAGES strategy may be used while listening or reading. It has five parts:

P= Pause and Picture
A= Ask Questions
G = Go Back or Go Forward
E = Explore Words
S = Summarize

What's the Big Idea – Students work on distinguishing between the main idea and supporting details. This activity is also available on Boom Cards for an additional fee.

Struggling readers often get left out of rich writing opportunities. Even after decoding skills improve, struggling readers may still lag behind their peers in written language development. It is important to scaffold the advanced written responses below and provide adequate support so that written language goals are both challenging and attainable.

Comprehension Questions - Many older students are expected to answer questions using a RACE format or something similar. Many struggling learners need this process broken down into manageable steps and modeled. After reading or listening to each section of the Background Information from *Hank the Tank*, students answer comprehension questions by restating the question before providing the answer. Many students with writing challenges will need the additional support of being able to answer verbally or of using a voice-to-text option to create written responses. That's okay. They are still learning the grade level expectations and are growing in their ability to give more detailed answers.

RACE Responses - Students ready for complete RACE Responses may add to their answers above by citing evidence from the text and further explaining their answers. Students with learning differences may need the selection read aloud for them a second or third time.

PAGES

Use this strategy when reading or listening to something read aloud.

Picture – Pause after a **period**, a **paragraph**, or a **page** of text and try to form a mental **picture** of what you have just read.

Ask – There are many questions you might **ask** yourself about what you have read, but the first and most important two are, "Was I able to form a picture?" and "Does that picture make sense?" You may also **ask** clarification questions and questions about Who is Doing What? Also, **ask** yourself if there are words that you don't know or that don't make sense.

Go Back or Go Forward – Do you need to **go back** and reread what you just read? Sometimes you need to keep moving **forward**. A confusing word or reference may become clearer in the next sentence or when you finish the sentence you are reading.

Explore words - Are there unfamiliar **words** that are explained in the context or that need to be looked up in the dictionary?

Summarize – Once the above steps have been taken, put the information into your own words. If you are not ready to **summarize**, you may need to go back and explore some of the steps again.

What's the Big Idea

based on *Hank the Tank*
by Carolee Dean

Directions: Circle the letter that represents the main idea. These cards May be cut out and used as game cards. They are also available as Boom Cards.

A. Black bears can be black.
B. Black bears can be a variety of colors.
C. Black bears can be brown.
D. Black bears can even be white.

A. Eating trash can make wild animals sick.
B. There are many reasons why people who live in resort areas should pick up their trash.
C. Trash pollutes the environment.
D. Trash attracts bears.

A. Grizzly bears have a hump.
B. Grizzly bears have longer claws.
C. Grizzly fur may be grizzled.
D. There are many differences between black bears and grizzly bears.

A. When a bear climbs into a trap, a metal door closes behind it.
B. During a Trap, Tag, and Haze operation, game wardens first set up traps.
C. Officers tranquilize the bear.
D. Officers put an ear tag on the bear.

A. Game wardens use hazing to discourage bears from interacting with humans.
B. Officers open the door to let the bear out of the trap.
C. Officers make loud, annoying sounds.
D. Officers may shoot bean bags at the bear.

A. A snarling dog may look like a coyote to a bear.
B. Dogs sometimes chase bears.
C. Dogs sometimes corner bears.
D. Bears do not like dogs for several reasons.

A. There are several reasons why people should never feed bears.
B. Humans carry diseases that may be dangerous to bears.
C. In many places, it is illegal to feed wild animals.
D. When bears get used to human food, they will eat trash.

A. Bears can be similar in size and color.
B. A bear's weight can change drastically over the year.
C. Identifying a specific bear can be difficult.
D. Unless bears have markings, it can be hard to tell them apart.

A. Fruit should be picked up and not left on the ground to rot.
B. Bears can open doors, so people should lock their cars.
C. People can co-exist peacefully with bears if they do a few simple things.
D. It's important to keep trash in a secure container.

A. Relocating problem bears is not always a good solution.
B. Relocated bears often try to find their way back home.
C. Bears can be hit by cars.
D. Hunting for food in a new location can be a challenge for bears.

What's the Big Idea
based on *Hank the Tank*
by Carolee Dean

ANSWERS

A. Black bears can be black.
B. Black bears can be a variety of colors.
C. Black bears can be brown.
D. Black bears can even be white.

A. Eating trash can make wild animals sick.
B. There are many reasons why people who live in resort areas should pick up their trash.
C. Trash pollutes the environment.
D. Trash attracts bears.

A. Grizzly bears have a hump.
B. Grizzly bears have longer claws.
C. Grizzly fur may be grizzled.
D. There are many differences between black bears and grizzly bears.

A. When a bear climbs into a trap, a metal door closes behind it.
B. During a Trap, Tag, and Haze operation, game wardens first set up traps.
C. Officers tranquilize the bear.
D. Officers put an ear tag on the bear.

A. Game wardens use hazing to discourage bears from interacting with humans.
B. Officers open the door to let the bear out of the trap.
C. Officers make loud, annoying sounds.
D. Officers may shoot bean bags at the bear.

A. A snarling dog may look like a coyote to a bear.
B. Dogs sometimes chase bears.
C. Dogs sometimes corner bears.
D. Bears do not like dogs for several reasons.

A. There are several reasons why people should never feed bears.
B. Humans carry diseases that may be dangerous to bears.
C. In many places, it is illegal to feed wild animals.
D. When bears get used to human food, they will eat trash.

A. Bears can be similar in size and color.
B. A bear's weight can change drastically over the year.
C. Identifying a specific bear can be difficult.
D. Unless bears have markings, it can be hard to tell them apart.

A. Fruit should be picked up and not left on the ground to rot.
B. Bears can open doors, so people should lock their cars.
C. People can co-exist peacefully with bears if they do a few simple things.
D. It's important to keep trash in a secure container.

A. Relocating problem bears is not always a good solution.
B. Relocated bears often try to find their way back home.
C. Bears can be hit by cars.
D. Hunting for food in a new location can be a challenge for bears.

Comprehension Questions about the Background Information

Directions:

1. READ the section that is specified for each question.

2. RESTATE the question on a separate piece of paper.

3. ANSWER the question in your own words in a complete sentence. Leave several blank lines between answers. You may need to come back later to add more information.

EXAMPLE

QUESTION: from WHO WAS THE REAL HANK? Why is naming and identifying bears problematic?

ANSWER: (answers will vary) Naming and identifying bears is problematic because bears can look very similar.

Questions:

1. From TRAP, TAG, AND HAZE
   Why do agents tag bears after they trap them?

2. From BLACK BEARS ARE NOT GRIZZLIES
   What is one way that black bears and grizzlies are different?

3. From FEAR OF HUMANS
   Why is it important for bears to keep their natural fear of humans?

4. from HIBERNATION
   What happens when bears go into hyperphagia?

5. From DOGS AND BEARS
   What is one way that humans can keep their dogs safe from bears?

6. From CAN BEARS AND HUMANS CO-EXIST
   Name one thing humans can do to live peacefully with bears.

7. From KEEP BEARS WILD
   Name one thing you can do to help keep bears wild.

Answers

for Comprehension Questions

Make sure students have restated the question and answered it in a complete sentence. Answers may vary.

1. Agents tag bears after they trap them so that they can track their location.

2. One way that black bears and grizzlies are different is that grizzlies have a hump between their shoulders and black bears do not.

3. It is important for bears to keep their natural fear of humans so that they will stay away from houses.

4. When bears go into hyperphagia, they eat a lot of food and put on weight.

5. One way that humans can keep their dogs safe from bears is to keep their pet on a sturdy leash.

6. One thing humans can do to live peacefully with bears is to keep the doors locked on their homes and cars.

7. One thing humans can do to help to keep bears wild is to never feed them.

RACE Responses

Directions: Go back to your answers for the Comprehension Questions. You should have already completed **R** and **A** below. Now add **C** and **E**. **Cite** the evidence and **Explain**.

R – Restate the question

A– Answer the question

C – Cite the evidence from the text to support your answer.

E – Explain your answer

EXAMPLE

QUESTION: from WHO WAS THE REAL HANK? Why is naming and identifying bears problematic?

ANSWER: (answers will vary) Naming and identifying bears is problematic because bears can look very similar. The text states, "Unless bears have specific markings, they can look very similar, and their weight can fluctuate quite a bit." People often mistake one bear for another, and this can result in a bear being blamed for something it did not do.

Graphic Organizers for Paragraph & Essay Writing

INTRODUCTION

The following graphic organizers and templates were designed to provide the building blocks needed to create paragraphs and essays.

Fun Facts – This simple template is for recording facts students hear or read from the Background Information section of *Hank the Tank*. It may also be used for topics they research on their own. They may use a separate page for each section of the book.

Alternate Endings – Many students have difficulty stating information in a different way when writing a conclusion. This activity focuses specifically on writing a conclusion by restating the introduction in different words, adding information, or creating a call to action.

What's the Big Idea - Revisit this activity from the Comprehension section. Students choose one group of sentences and rewrite them as a paragraph. Instruct them to start with the main idea, add the details using transition words, and add a conclusion.

ESSAY WRITING
The next three activities build upon each other

1. Venn Diagrams – Students brainstorm information needed for Compare and Contrast writing. Some students may only be ready for a discussion about the Venn Diagram. For those ready for a bigger challenge, use the information in the Venn Diagram for High Five Writing.

2. High Five Writing - Students incorporate the information from a Venn Diagram into one well-structured paragraph. Students may use the same template to construct more than one paragraph on the same topic. For those ready to tackle an essay, see the next activity.

3. I+P+P+C Compare & Contrast Essay Students follow the directions to incorporate those well-crafted paragraphs from High Five Writing into a multi-paragraph response.

Each level builds on the one before it. Remember to provide students with all the support they need to be successful at every step.

Fun Facts
based on *Hank the Tank*
by Carolee Dean

Subject: _____

Directions:
1. Write a subject at the top of the paper.
2. Make a list of Fun Facts about the subject.

Fun Facts

Alternate Endings & Conclusions

based on *Hank the Tank*
by Carolee Dean

Ron Riter does a pretty good job of stating a main idea and supporting it with details, but when it comes to writing a conclusion, all he does is restate the main idea. Help Ron by rewriting his conclusion in different words. You can expand on the information in the paragraph, connect it to a related topic, or even create a call to action.

1. There are many reasons why people who live in resort areas should pick up their trash. Trash pollutes the environment. It contaminates lakes and ponds. It makes beautiful natural areas ugly. Most important, when wild animals eat trash, it can make them sick. Unsecured trash cans encourage animals to get dangerously close to humans. **There are many reasons why people who live in resort areas should pick up their trash.**

Rewrite the concluding sentence here: _____

_____

_____

2. People can co-exist peacefully with bears if they do a few simple things. It's important to keep trash in a secure container and not put it out until trash day. Fruit should be picked and not left to rot on the ground. In addition, bears can open doors, so it is important to lock houses and cars. **People can co-exist peacefully with bears if they do a few simple things.**

Rewrite the concluding sentence here: _____

_____

_____

 # Big Idea Paragraphs
based on *Hank the Tank*
by Carolee Dean

DIRECTIONS:

1. Choose one group of sentences and rewrite it as a paragraph below.
2. Start with the main idea which is in bold. Add the details.
3. Use at least three transition words (first, second, next, then, in addition, also, as a result, furthermore, finally, etc).
4. End with a conclusion by expanding on the information in the paragraph, connecting it to a related topic, or even creating a call to action. Use more paper if needed.

A. **Black bears can be a variety of colors.**
B. Black bears can be black.
C. Black bears can be brown.
D. Black bears can even be white.

A. **There are several reasons why people should never feed bears.**
B. Humans carry diseases that may be dangerous to bears.
C. In many places, it is illegal to feed wild animals.
D. When bears get used to human food, they will eat trash.

A. **Game wardens use hazing to discourage bears from interacting with humans.**
B. Officers open the door to let the bear out of the trap.
C. Officers make loud, annoying sounds.
D. Officers may shoot bean bags at the bear.

A. **Relocating problem bears is not always a good solution.**
B. Relocated bears often try to find their way back home.
C. Bears can be hit by cars.
D. Hunting for food in a new location can be a challenge for bears.

_____

_____

_____

_____

_____

_____

Venn Diagram
based on *Hank the Tank*
by Carolee Dean

Directions:
1. Read or listen to "Black Bears Are Not Grizzlies."
2. List the ways that black bears and grizzlies are the same.
3. List the ways that black bears and grizzlies are different.

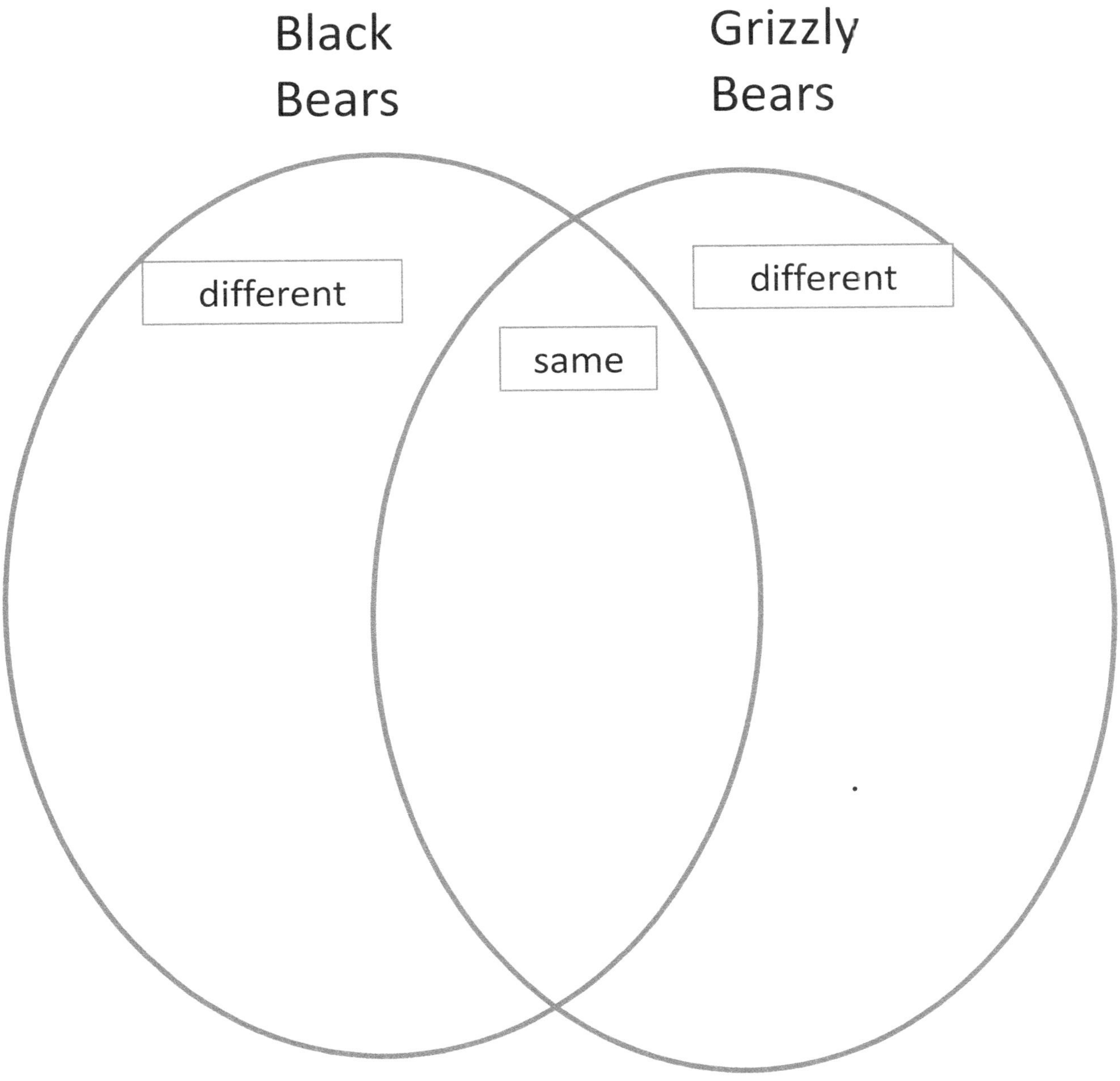

Black
Bears

Grizzly
Bears

different

different

same

Venn Diagram

based on *Hank the Tank*
by Carolee Dean

Directions:

1. Stories and Informational Texts can be quite different. *Hank the Tank* includes a section of Informational Text or Background Information that comes after the story.
2. List the ways that the story and the background section are similar.
3. List the ways they are different.

Story Poem   Background Information

different

different

same

Venn Diagram
based on *Hank the Tank*
by Carolee Dean

Directions:
1. Choose a narrative and an informational text on the same subject. You may want to use *Backyard Bears* by Amy Cherrix and compare it to *Hank the Tank.*
2. List the ways that the books are different.
3. List the ways they are the same.

Narrative:
Hank the Tank

Informational Text:
Backyard Bears

different

different

same

High Five Paragraph Writing

Directions:

1. Use the *High Five Writing* template on the next page to brainstorm the **differences** between black bears and grizzlies. Write a paragraph.

2. Next, brainstorm and write a paragraph about the **similarities** between black bears and grizzlies. Use extra paper if needed.

_____

_____

_____

_____

_____

_____

_____

_____

_____

_____

High Five Writing Brainstorm

By Carolee Dean, M.S., CCC-SLP, CALT

Write a paragraph based on the format below:

Write a 1-2 sentence INTRODUCTION:

Describe three or more supporting details in three or more separate sentences.

Write a conclusion.

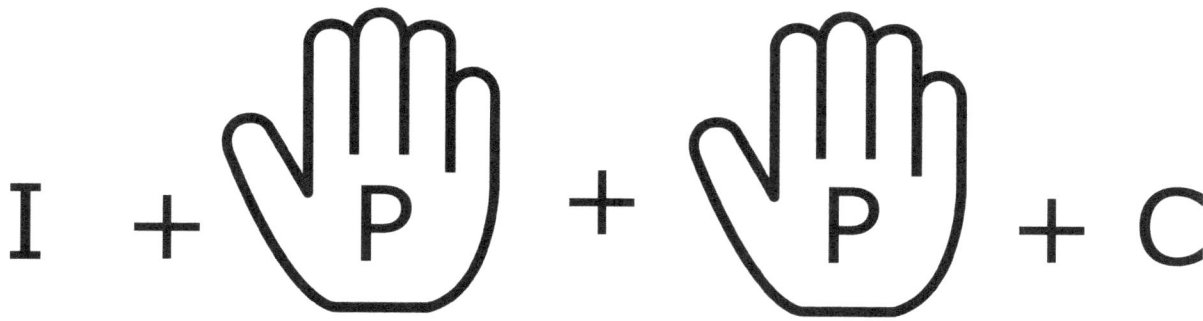

Compare & Contrast Essay

Note: Complete the brainstorms for paragraphs 2 and 3 using the *High Five Writing Brainstorm* **before** writing the introduction (paragraph 1).

Directions:

1. **Paragraph 1** – Write an **introduction** explaining in a general way why some people may confuse black bears with grizzlies. Give hints about why this is not true, but don't give too many details.

2. **Paragraph 2** - Use the paragraph that you wrote for the *High Five Writing Brainstorm* to discuss how black bears are **similar** to grizzlies. Refine your ideas. Add details and descriptive words. Add transition words between paragraphs.

3. **Paragraph 3** – Use the paragraph that you wrote for the *High Five Writing Brainstorm* to discuss how black bears and grizzlies are **different**. Refine your ideas. Add details and descriptive words. Add transition words between paragraphs.

4. **Paragraph 4** – Write a **conclusion** stating why it is important not to confuse black bears with grizzlies.

5. **EDIT** – Go back through your essay to check spelling and punctuation. Make sure there are smooth transitions between the paragraphs.

CREATE

INTRODUCTION

CREATE is the highest level of Bloom's Revised Taxonomy because it requires a student to synthesize what has been learned and reorganize the information into something new. Within this domain, activities move from concrete to abstract and from factual to conceptual, then procedural, and finally metacognitive. A list of activities along this continuum is found below.

A. **Factual**: Students make a list of suggestions for keeping bears away from your home or campsite using the *Helpful Tips* sheet. Turn your list into an information poster.

B. **Conceptual**: Students create a drawing or diorama about one of the scenes from the story. Write a paragraph describing the setting.

C. **Procedural**: Students go back to the *Snack Attack Word Mash-Up* from the Vocabulary Section. If you have not done so, create a snack food by combining two different foods. Then write a recipe with step-by-step directions for how to create your snack.

D. **Metacognitive**: In the story of *Goldilocks and the Three Bears*, a girl breaks into the home of three bears. She eats their porridge, breaks a chair, and falls asleep in one of their beds. The story of *Hank the Tank* involves three bears breaking into houses. Students write a mash-up of these two stories where three bears visit Goldilocks. Ask students to consider if it is easier for them to create a completely original story or to create a spoof of an existing story.

BEAR TIPS
Information Poster
based on *Hank the Tank*
by Carolee Dean

Subject: _____

Directions:
1. Pick a subject for staying safe in bear country like *Tips for Hikers, Be Bear Aware*, *Keep Bears Wild*, or *Camping Safety.*
2. On a separate piece of paper, use your Helpful Tips to create an information poster.

Helpful Tips

Setting Description
based on *Hank the Tank*
by Carolee Dean

Directions:
1. Draw a scene from the story on a separate piece of paper or create a 3-D diorama.
2. Write a paragraph describing the setting.

SETTING DESCRIPTION:

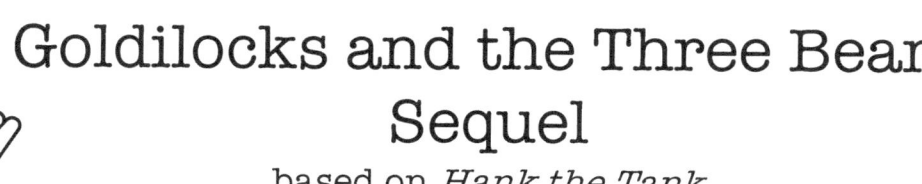

Goldilocks and the Three Bears Sequel

based on *Hank the Tank*
by Carolee Dean

Directions:
Use the prompts below to brainstorm ideas for your story. On a separate piece of paper, write your spoof.

1. In the original story of Goldilocks and the three bears, the bears go for a walk to let their porridge cool. Think of a reason why Goldilocks and her family have left their home for a few hours. Write that reason below.

2. Imagine that Mama Bear, Papa Bear, and Baby Bear break into Goldilocks' house. Use your knowledge of bears to describe why they choose her house and how they get inside.

3. Use your knowledge of bears to describe what the bears do while they are in the house.

4. Use your knowledge of bears to describe how Goldilocks and her family react to finding three bears in their house.

Write a Story
based on *Hank the Tank*
by Carolee Dean

Directions:
Use your brainstorm on the previous page to write a story below. Think of a funny title. Use additional paper if you need it.

Title:_____

Downloads & Online Resources

Activity Pages PDF Download

Free with the Purchase of the *Hank the Tank Activity Book*
The download includes:
5 Game Boards
15 Pages of Flash Cards for Articulation and/or Reading Practice
40+ Reproducible Activity Pages
Links to Virtual Dice

To Access the Activity Pages PDF Download,
go to www.wordtravelpress.com
Visit the Page for *Hank the Tank* (Look under Level 2 Products)
Enter the Purchaser's Password – **BearsR2Cool**

Boom Cards

Several virtual Boom Card decks/games are available for FREE at
Boom Learning where you may set up a free account:
Target Word Flash Cards
Virtual Game Board
Sound Tracker
Cognitive Flexibility Game

Other games found in the Activity Book have been turned into
Boom Cards that may be played online for a small additional fee.

Go to https://wow.boomlearning.com
Search for **Store>Word Travel Press.**

**If you have any issues with access, contact
info@wordtravelpress.com**

HOT Topics

HOT Topics (Page 1)
Hank the Tank by Carolee Dean
(Based on Bloom's Revised Taxonomy)
https://wordtravelpress.com/

Introduction: The following list of activities is from the decodable book, *Hank the Tank Activity Book*(from Level 2 of the HOT ROD Series). Activities have been designed to support Higher Order Thinking Skills and are arranged according to Bloom's Revised Taxonomy. These are only examples. Other activities may also apply to the various categories.

1. REMEMBER: Recall Details
A. **Factual**: Read or listen to a section from the Background Information. Use the *Fun Facts* template to write down interesting details.
B. **Conceptual**: Restate questions and answer them for RACE responses.
C. **Procedural**: Using a blank piece of paper, draw a series of stick figures to show the action of the story using the pictography strategy described in the Story Frames section.
D. **Metacognitive**: Before reading the story, share prior knowledge about bears through a class discussion or a written response. Discuss preconceived ideas and beliefs about bears that break into houses. Prepare for the idea that some of the preconceived ideas may be true and some may not.

2. UNDERSTAND: Make Meaning
A. **Factual**: Copy the words and definitions from WOW Vocabulary onto index cards and study them. Play a memory-matching game.
B. **Conceptual**: Study the Multiple Meaning Words. Then play a memory-matching game. Be careful not to confuse similar words with each other.
C. **Procedural**: Follow the directions to create the *Vocabulary Foldable*.
D. **Metacognitive**: Test yourself using the WOW Vocabulary foldable or index cards. Predict how accurate you will be before you start. Then tally your correct and incorrect responses. How accurate were you at predicting your performance?

Hank the Tank by Carolee Dean
(Based on Bloom's Revised Taxonomy)
https://wordtravelpress.com/

3. APPLY: Use Information for a Task

A. **Factual**: Use the stick figure drawings from 1C to complete a storyboard. Use the storyboard to retell the story or write a summary.

B. **Conceptual**: Rewrite conclusions for the *Alternate Endings* activity.

C. **Procedural**: Complete *Sentence Construction #1- Sentence Combining*. Use conjunctions to combine short sentences.

D. **Metacognitive**: Use the PAGES strategy to check your understanding as you read. How often are you able to form a picture of what you have read? Do you use the strategy of going back to reread?

4. ANALYZE: Compare Parts to the Whole

A. **Factual**: Using Morpho Mania #3, study the words that contain the root *tract*. Then reread the section on "Dogs and Bears" and the section on "Can Bears and Humans Co-exist?" Make a tally of how many times you find each word.

B. **Conceptual**: *Complete Sentence Construction #3 - Identifying Complete Sentences.* Determine if sentences are complete or incomplete. Then decide if the sentence is missing a subject or a predicate.

C. **Procedural**: Follow the direction to complete *Feel the Beat* by drawing a drumstick above the stressed syllables.

D. **Metacognitive**: Determine which words go together in Rhyme Time #1. Circle words that rhyme and underline alliterations. Then write sentences. Think about how you tackle tasks. Would rather complete all three steps for each word before moving on OR would you prefer to do all the rhymes first, then all the alliterations, and then all the sentences? Is this how you usually work?

5. EVALUATE: Use Criteria to Make Judgements

A. **Factual**: Make a list of characteristics of black bears and grizzlies.

B. **Conceptual**: Complete a *Venn Diagram* by comparing and contrasting black bears and grizzlies.

C. **Procedural**: Use the High Five template to write a paragraph about ways black bears and grizzlies are different. Write another paragraph about their similarities.

D. **Metacognitive**: Discuss if previous ideas about bears have changed since reading the book.

6. CREATE: Reorganize Information into Something New

A. **Factual**: Make a list of suggestions for keeping bears away from your home or campsite using the *Helpful Tips* sheet. Turn your list into an information poster.
B. **Conceptual**: Create a drawing or diorama based on one of the scenes from the story.
C. **Procedural**: Go back to the *Snack Attack Word Mash-Up* from the Vocabulary Section. If you have not done so, create a snack food by combining two different foods. Then write a recipe with step-by-step directions for how to create your snack.
D. **Metacognitive**: In the story of *Goldilocks and the Three Bears*, a girl breaks into the home of three bears. She eats their porridge, breaks a chair, and falls asleep in one of their beds. The story of *Hank the Tank* involves three bears breaking into houses. Write a mash-up of these two stories where three bears visit Goldilocks. Consider if it is easier for you to create a completely original story or to create a spoof of an existing story.

Read more about the **HOT ROD** (**H**igher **O**rder **T**hinking through the **R**eading **o**f **D**ecodables) **Series** at https://wordtravelpress.com/

Reference:
Anderson, L.W., & Krathwohl, D. R. (Eds.). (2001). *A taxonomy for learning, teaching, and assessing: A revision of Bloom's taxonomy of educational objectives*. New York, NY: Addison Wesley Longman, Inc.

References

Anderson, L.W., & Krathwohl, D. R. (Eds.). (2001). *A taxonomy for learning, teaching, and assessing: A revision of Bloom's taxonomy of educational objectives.* New York, NY: Addison Wesley Longman, Inc.

Davidson, B., & Liben, D. (2019) What a knowledge-building approach looks like in the classroom. *Perspectives on Language and Literacy*, 45 (4), 31-35

Dean, C. (2021). *Story frames for teaching literacy: Enhancing student learning through the power of storytelling.* Baltimore, MD: Paul H. Brookes Publishing Co.

Duchan, J.F. (2004). The Foundational role of schemas in children's language and literacy learning. In Stone, C.A, Sillman, E.R., Ehren B.J., & Apel, K. (Eds.), *Handbook of language and literacy.* (pp. 380-397). New York: The Guilford Press

Cartwright, K.B. (2023). *Executive skills and reading comprehension: A guide for educators* (Second Edition). New York, NY: Guildford Press.

Farrell, L.M., & Cushen-Whte, N. (2018). Structured literacy instruction . In J.R. Birsh & S. Carreker (Eds.) *Multisensory teaching of basic language skills* (4th ed., pp. 35-72). Baltimore, MD: Paul H. Brookes Publishing Co.

Green, L. B., & Klecan-Aker, J. S. (2012). Teaching story grammar components to increase oral narrative ability: A group intervention study. *Child Language Teaching and Therapy*, 28, 263–276.

Hochman, J.C. & MacDermott-Duffy, B. (2018). Composition: Evidence-based instruction. In J.R. Birsh & S. Carreker (Eds.) *Multisensory teaching of basic language skills* (4th ed., pp. 646-676 Baltimore, MD: Paul H. Brookes Publishing Co.

Kilpatrick, D.A. (2016). Equipped for reading success: A comprehensive, step-by-step program for developing phonemic awareness and fluent word recognition. Syracuse, NY: Casey & Kirsch Publishers.

Nelson, N.W. (2013). Syntax development in the school-age years: implications for assessment and intervention. *Perspectives on Language and Literacy*. 39 (3), 9-15.

Tunmer, W.E., & Chapman, J.W. (2012). Does set for variability mediate the influence of vocabulary knowledge on the development of word recognition skills? *Scientific Studies of Reading*, 16(2), 122-140.

Paulson, L. H. (2018). Teaching phonemic awareness. In J.R. Birsh & S. Carreker (Eds.) *Multisensory teaching of basic language skills* (4th ed., pp. 205-253). Baltimore, MD: Paul H. Brookes Publishing Co.

Scott, C.M., & Balthazar, C. (2013). The role of complex sentence knowledge in children with reading and writing difficulties. *Perspectives on Language and Literacy. 39* (3), 18-26.

Shanahan, T. (2015). Are you lactating? On the importance of academic language. *Perspectives on Language and Literacy, 41*(3), 14-16.

Shanahan, T. (2019). Why children should be taught to read with more challenging texts. *Perspectives on Language and Literacy, 45*(4), 17-23.

Stein, N., & Glenn, C. (1979). An analysis of story comprehension in elementary school children. In R. Freedle (Ed.), New directions in discourse processing (Vol. 2, pp. 53-120). Norwood, NJ: Ablex.

Ukrainetz, T. (1998). Stickwriting stories: A quick and easy narrative representation strategy. *Language, Speech, and Hearing in Schools*, 29, 197-206.

Vadasy, P.F., Sanders, E.A., Cartwright, K.B. (2022). Cognitive flexibility in beginning decoding and encoding. *The Journal of Education for Students Placed at Risk.*

Van Cleave, W. (2014). *Writing matters: Developing sentence skills in students of all ages (Second Edition).* Greenville, SC: W.V.C.ED.

Wright, T.S., & Neuman, S.B. (2015). The power of content-rich vocabulary instruction. *Perspectives on Language and Literacy*, 41 (3), 25-28.

Zipke, M. (2016). The importance of flexibility of pronunciation in learning to decode: A training study in set for variability. *First Language*. 36 (1), 71-86.

HOT ROD Titles

Watch for additional books from the HOT ROD series. Visit www.wordtravelpress.com

Level 1 – Closed syllables and consonant blends.

About Set 1: This set includes three colorful picture books that together form the Greek Creation Myth. They are separate books but work best as a set. Book 4 will be a black-and-white version of the three stories for older students. The decodable portion is the same as in Books 1-3 but Book 4 will include extensive background information.

Set 1, Book 1: *No Gift for Man* – Zeus asks Prometheus and his brother to fill the world with living creatures. Prometheus makes man. Epimetheus creates the animals and gives them all sorts of interesting gifts, but when man comes around for his gift, there is nothing left.

Set 1, Book 2: *The Bandit* - Prometheus steals fire from Mount Olympus to give to the humans and suffers the wrath of Zeus.

Set 1, Book 3: *The Box* – (coming fall 2023). Zeus gets revenge on mankind for accepting the gift of fire. The gods create Pandora, giving her many talents and charms. Then they send her to Epimetheus as a bride and give the couple a mysterious box they are told to never open.

Book 4: Gods and Gifts – (coming fall 2023) The same three stories above are told with black and white illustrations for older students and adults. Background information about the discovery of fire, additional creation myths, and other topics are included.

Level 2 – digraphs, trigraphs, combinations (ng, ck, sh, th, ch, tch, qu, wh) single consonant n=n(g)k, and suffix –ing.

Hank the Tank: Animal in the Spotlight – A bear's life is saved through science and DNA.

Level 3 – open syllables, consonant-le, suffix -ed

Raven Remix – (coming winter 2024) A fun mash-up of popular titles by Edgar Allen Poe told in the format of the story poem, "The Raven."

Visit www.wordtravelpress.com to find the Scope and Sequence of the series. Sign up for the monthly newsletter to keep up with book news, articles, and free activities.

UPDATE ON HANK

Back in the News

(with a name change)

According to the Wild Animal Sanctuary NEWS and an NPR Report from August, DNA evidence proved that one of the "Hanks" in the news in 2022 was a female, which the California Department of Fish and Wildlife (CDFW) identified as Bear 64F. By monitoring the bear with a tracking collar, authorities determined that she was responsible for 21 or more of the fifty bear invasions between California and Nevada in the Lake Tahoe Area. According to NPR, she spent the winter months in a den under a home in the Tahoe Keys.

Due to intense public support, the life of Bear 64F was spared. After being captured by CDFW in the summer of 2023, that agency, in collaboration with Colorado Parks and Wildlife, allowed The Wild Animal Sanctuary (TWAS) to transport the bear to a 230-acre Wild Animal Refuge outside of Springfield, CO. When she arrived, she got a beautiful new home and a new name – Henrietta. Unfortunately, this type of rescue is the exception rather than the rule. Hundreds of "nuisance bears" are euthanized every year, and places like TWAS can't possibly rescue all of them. Not only that but relocated bears tend to either try to find their way back home or wreak havoc in their new location.

The Wild Animal Refuge is a beautiful 230-acre wooded property in Colorado. Henrietta will receive plenty of food, so they are expecting she will be content to stay put. It is one of the properties belonging to The Wild Animal Sanctuary. Although visitors are not allowed at the Refuge, they are welcome and encouraged to visit the Wild Animal Sanctuary in Keenesburg, CO. It is located about 35 miles northeast of Denver and is open almost every day of the year. Ticket sales and donations help to support the mission of this important non-profit charity. If you can't visit in person, check out their website at www.WildAnimalSanctuary.org and read about other exciting animal rescues.